Rebellions and Wars

The Imperial Archives

FROM DISCOVERY TO THE CIVILISATIONAL MISSION: ENGLISH WRITINGS ON INDIA

Volume 4

Rebellions and Wars

Editor

Pramod K. Nayar

B L O O M S B U R Y

NEW DELHI • LONDON • OXFORD • NEW YORK • SYDNEY

BLOOMSBURY INDIA
Bloomsbury Publishing India Pvt. Ltd
Second Floor, LSC Building No. 4, DDA Complex, Pocket C – 6 & 7,
Vasant Kunj, New Delhi, 110070

BLOOMSBURY, BLOOMSBURY ACADEMIC INDIA and the Diana logo are trademarks of Bloomsbury Publishing Plc

First published in India 2022
This edition published 2022

Bloomsbury Academic
An imprint of Bloomsbury Publishing Plc

ISBN: HB: 978-93-54358-31-9; ePDF: 978-93-54359-10-1
2 4 6 8 10 9 7 5 3 1

Printed & bound in India by Replika Press Pvt. Ltd.

CONTENTS

PREFATORY NOTE

The archival texts have been retained in their original font, style and content in order to clearly show the environment of the time when these documents were produced. It is important to show in a book such as this the views held at that time and the profound effect they had on society. We acknowledge that several of the texts are derogatory about Indians, women and communities of different religious faiths like many hundreds of other colonial-era-based works. While these are clearly unacceptable to us today, we have not attempted to change any wording or redact the texts so that the contemporary reader may experience the rhetoric, attitude and ideologies that so clearly marked the Raj. In places, where the text had been smudged and rendered impossible to read, that specific segment has been deleted.

We would like to make clear that these are not the views held by the editor or Bloomsbury India and do not reflect our mission and values which are clearly stated on our website (https://www.bloomsbury.com/in/connect/about-us/missions-and-values/)

GENERAL INTRODUCTION: ARCHIVE AND EMPIRE

That the British writings on India occupy over several miles of shelf space in the British Library, London, is an apocryphal tale, but one which *may* have substance, given that there was no aspect of the subcontinent that did not pique the curiosity of the British or generate some document or the other.

In his *The Imperial Archive: Knowledge and the Fantasy of Empire* (1993), Thomas Richards demonstrated how the documentation (the subject of considerable work, notably in Bernard Cohn and others) and archivisation not only produced knowledge about the colonies but were also instrumental in generating the fantasy of absolute control. And yet, it is never easy to read these records produced by a diverse set of English, Irish and Scottish missionaries, administrators, men of leisure, nurses, teachers, wives and/or sisters of the men who occupied official posts in the colony, soldiers, mercenaries and others—many of whom, for many reasons, had their own dynamics and tensions with the *English*.

Several approaches to the imperial record exist, and this introductory chapter sets out some of them.[1] In the process, it also flags what the archive does in terms of the imperial structure and processes.[2]

The Power of the Archive

The archive is not a mere compilation of what John Malcolm (1823) advised his officers on the right approach to the native officers, or what Thomas Williamson (1808) described as the potential for the hunt in India. The archive is not a passive reflection of imperial power—it constitutes and constructs it. As diverse commentators—such as Cohn's work on the 'survey modality' (1997) and C.A. Bayly's *Empire and Information* (1999)—have pointed out, the Empire ran on information,

---

[1] I use the term 'imperial archive' throughout to refer to the corpus of published material across genres, as diverse as maps, geographical accounts, census reports, travelogues, administrative reports, ecclesiastical documents.

[2] These volumes work only with the print archive of British India, although a vast archive of visual material also exists, and has been the subject of significant studies. See, for example, Guégan (2011), Chaudhury (2012), Pinney (2014), Dohman (2017) on colonial photography, and Tobin (1999), De Silva (2011), Eaton (2013), among others, on colonial/imperial art and paintings.

and information-gathering constituted not just an act of power but was a *constituent* of the power structure. It classified, organised and legislated on the subject peoples, through the census, the geographies and anthropological studies. In the process, it defined who is counted as a subject/citizen. For instance, writing about the Todas or the Gonds, and then examining the numbers of Muslim students in schools, both the educationist and the statesman were constructing model imperial citizens who would benefit, resist or accept from 'modern' education. In other words, the imperial archive on education was not merely advocating 'modern' education: it was constructing *educate-able* citizens from among their colonial subjects while abandoning the others. Thus, archivisation and informatisation were ultimately about the power wielded over the identity-making and rights of the subjects.[3]

Relatedly, the archive and the documentation also made the subjects *visible to themselves*. With 'modern' education, for instance, the Indian colonial subject in school or college came to identify themselves in particular ways. They learnt what it means to be a good citizen, to be modern, to develop and demand certain skills, etc. They recognised their location on the civilisational scale in the books they read and assimilated (*primitive* and *non-modern* as opposed to the modern European). In an argument that resonates with my claims above, Antoinette Burton and Isabel Hofmeyr write about the power of the English book:

> The embodiment of English manly authority, the book was not simply 'a surrogate Englishman in his highest and most perfect state,' it was the very emblem of imperial sovereignty—with the rigorous spine a testimony to its singularity, its probity, its titular power … books impressed themselves in the everyday lives of imperial subjects, manifesting the formal values of an elite or bourgeois self and modeling in their material form the coherence and commanding presence of British imperial power itself. (2014: 1–2)

The colonial subjects were told, through these English books, what kind of spiritual and moral training was required for them to 'improve'.

[3] It must be noted that it was not only the human subjects in the colony that became objects and subjects of the imperial archive. Fauna and flora, climate, landscape and topography—indeed the natural world in its entirety—were also archived. For studies, see Edney (1997) and Damodaran et al. (2015), among others.

As A.H. Benton of the Indian Civil Service wrote in *Indian Moral Instruction and Caste Problems*:

> [The Indian] People are on the whole kindly, docile, alert, keen-spirited, high and low, one of the best-mannered peoples in the world, and they would appear to offer a very promising field for right spiritual treatment. (1917: 92)

The education archive, and especially its insistence on moral training and moral apprenticeship of the subjects as a *preliminary* to training for political citizenship, was built on the

> founding assumption … that the native readership of English texts, and the recipients of English education, were amenable to their teachings, which led them to abandon their traditional manners and disciplines. This necessitated a solid moral training to make them good citizens. (Nayar 2020: 142)

The archive also, frequently, captures the rift and fracture within the colonial subject's responses to, say, Western/English education. See, for instance, Syed Mahmood's anguish about the Indian Muslim's refusal to accept this education:

> Such feelings of aversion towards English education entertained by the Mahomedans … stand in sharp contrast to the attitude of the Hindu community…. This difference in the sentiments of the two communities towards English education, is the real key to the reasons of the vast disparity of progress of English education which the two nationalities have respectively made. The effects of this disparity have been most baneful to the interests of British India in general, and to the Mahomedan community in particular. (1895: 23)

In time, the colonial subject, convinced of the 'truth' in the power of the Englishman's word or photographic record, not only accepted the arguments about their inferiority but also welcomed the interventions in the form of the civilisational mission of the Empire. The archive had, therefore, produced the *willing* colonial subject.

In particular cases, such as Thuggee, the archive enabled the colonial structures of law enforcement and the judiciary to enact legislation and, in the process, demonise specific cultural practices. Examining the Thuggee archive, Alexander Macfie writes:

> [W]hereas Sleeman and his colleagues tended to define the activities of the thugs in terms of wickedness, murder, deceit, cowardice and criminality, the thugs themselves tended to evaluate them in terms of courage, enterprise, bravery, daring, cunning, adventure and martial

> skill ... in terms usually associated by both the British and the Indians with the heroic values of war. (2008: 396)

The Archive, the Coloniser, the Colonised and Cultural Exchanges

Shifting focus, Antoinette Burton has demonstrated how the imperial archive also fed into the coloniser's psyche, imagination and political imagination. A pithy summary of how the imperial corpus fuelled, inspired and controlled the social imaginary, policies, attitudes and responses of the Britons in the nineteenth century is available in Burton's *Empire in Question*. Victorian culture, writes Burton,

> as a racialized landscape shaped by decades, if not centuries, of colonial peoples, goods, and ideas coursing through its highways and byways ... as always already imperial not just implicitly but as part of a pedagogical meta-narrative about the relationship of modernity to the world-historical phenomenon of colonialism in world history.... (2011: 2–3)

Burton proposes that English 'sensibility' was shaped by Britain's imperial role and character, and its concomitant racialised hierarchies—thus makes the production and consumption of texts (and commodities) about and from the colonised peripheries central to the making of Britain itself (also see Hall 2002).

The archive also instantiates, other than the racialised power binaries (white/black, coloniser/colonised), cross-cultural *influences* and *exchanges*. Contacts across races, ethnic groups and the coloniser–colonised divide were frequent through the colonial period.

The English language took into itself words from their colonial subjects. They also sought to document the grammars of the languages of the subcontinent for their own officers and staff. As a consequence, a vibrant field of cultural exchanges opened up in the languages, with Indian pandits and English philologists and grammarians collaborating. The imperial archive in this domain shows mutual influences of English on Indian languages and vice versa (including Sanskrit [Naregal 2001]) but also the *organisation* of knowledge around the latter (Lelyveld 1993; Rao 2004; Mir 2010; Auer 2014).[4] Scholars—the famous 'Orientalists'—translated texts from, say, Sanskrit into English. Organisations and societies, such as the Asiatic Society, the

[4] A detailed annotated bibliography on these and other aspects of English colonial discourse on India can be found in Nayar 2021.

Zoological Survey of India, the Archaeological Survey of India, were spaces through which the English statesman, *memsahib* and trader encountered Indian temples, art, food practices, superstitions, systems of healing, among others.

English literary texts, as numerous commentators have shown (Leask 1993; Teltscher 1997), began to introduce Indian 'themes' and motifs, whether the *sati* or the wealth of the country's landscape. This field of literary studies was one of contestation and adaptation (Vishwanathan 1990). Be that as it may, the circulation of the English novel in nineteenth-century India catered to the Indian audience attuned to the melodramatic and informed their own creative work (Joshi 2003). Other commentators like Harish Trivedi (1993) have noted how English literature was received in India and the transactional nature of this reception.

Local experts, *writers* and translators were an integral component of the East India Company and the British government. Even account and trade books were produced through a collaborative project (Ogborn 2007). In other domains, such as translations, Indian scholars like Kasinatha Bhattacharya enabled the work of Charles Wilkins (Davis 2015).

Manners, protocols of civic interaction and norms of social, interracial interaction were also sites where cultural exchange and mutual influence were visible. Even the idea of 'civility', as Anindyo Roy has argued, was treated by the native—and projected as such by *English* textbooks and teachers—as markers of 'modern progress and mobility' (Roy 2005: 11). Therefore, both English and Indian commentators (Webb 1915; El Edroos 1922) produced advice and courtesy books for Indians and Englishmen in India (Nayar 2016, 'Civil Modernity'). These contained suggestions like:

> Members of each class, without entering into political or official discussions and avoiding personal remarks, may have much pleasant intercourse by asking about and describing the manners and customs peculiar to each other's nationality, or about their art, music, poetry and literature.... Talk about sport is most suitable at club. (El Edroos: 89)

The Archive and the Global

Another approach to the imperial archive chooses to see the archive as instantiating not just the sensibilities, attitudes and modes of the British coloniser and the subcontinent's colonised, but as enabling *global and globalising imperial networks*. That is, the archive is seen as embodying not just the binary of an imperial 'centre' and 'periphery' (the colony), but a vast network of global connections. We see this interpretation in the work of John Darwin.

In *The Empire Project: The Rise and Fall of the British World-System, 1830–1970* (2009), Darwin shows how the 'interdependence' of various regions and colonies shaped the British Empire in four specific domains. First, there is the military interdependence of various geopolitical regions:

> the most obvious forms of such inter-dependence were naval and military.... British ability to provide naval protection or to send reinforcements to the scene of a conflict would have been very limited without the resources the imperial system supplied. It was strategic control of the Cape Colony (whose economic value was derisory before 1870) that secured the naval gateway to Asia from European waters. The prime function of Egypt, occupied by the British in 1882, was to preserve British use of the Suez Canal and protect the 'Clapham Junction' of imperial communications. Malta, Aden, Ceylon, Singapore, Hong Kong, Esquimalt (on Vancouver Island), the Falklands and Halifax, Nova Scotia, formed the network of bases from which the Royal Navy patrolled the world's sea-lanes. India played several roles in the British world-system, but perhaps its critical function was to be the main base from which British interests in Asia could be advanced and defended. Indian soldiers and a British garrison paid for by Indian revenues were the 'strategic reserve' of the British system in Asia. Because India played this role, other British possessions and spheres east and south of Suez were largely exempted from the costs of defence—a fact of crucial importance to their economic viability. (3–4)

Then there is the commercial interdependence and linkages:

> Both colonial territories and 'informal' colonies had to compete for investment and credits from London to expand their economies ... with the grand exception of the United States (which had received one-fifth of British foreign investment by 1913), British capital was shuttled by the City of London between the various sectors of its commercial empire (a vast global realm among whose key provinces were Canada, Argentina, India, Australia, Southern Africa, China and the Middle East), employing a calculus of prospective return and speculative gain. (4)

The third domain of such connections would be the demographic interdependence:

> Although two-thirds of British migrants went to the United States up until 1900, almost all the rest were distributed between the four main settlement zones of Canada, Australia, New Zealand and South Africa. Indeed, their economic development was usually seen as being closely dependent upon drawing labour and skills from the British supply.… Between 1834 and 1937, India exported some 30 million people to other British possessions as indentured labour, and perhaps one-fifth remained as permanent settlers. In the tropical empire (which British migrants avoided) they supplied much of the labour and business expertise to promote commercial expansion. (4–5)

Finally,

> the spheres of British expansion were progressively linked by a complex system of communication. From the 1840s onwards, this was provided by subsidised mail services, telegraph wires, undersea cables, an expanding rail network, fast passenger steamers and (in the twentieth century) imperial air routes. (5)

In consonance with the work of Darwin, other commentators have mapped these global connections and interdependencies of the British Empire. Thus, Tony Ballantyne, Jonathan Hyslop, among others, in their contributions to the *New Imperial Histories Reader*, map racial imaginings and knowledge formations, working-class presences across the Empire, from India to Australia and Southern Africa. The migration of people and goods in the 1850–1914 period, argue Gary Magee and Andrew Thompson in *Empire and Globalisation: Networks of People, Goods and Capital in the British World, c. 1850–1914* (2010), was instrumental in the making of an international economy. This, of course, put tremendous pressure on the colonised peoples but also made '"transnationalism"—living in and identifying with more than one country or place—a normal way of life for many British people in the half-century before 1914' (5); an argument that resonates with that of Antoinette Burton about Victorian England cited earlier.

Alan Lester's work in the field of imperial humanitarianism and the 'civilisational mission' has made similar connections to argue for a trans-imperial history. Through the late eighteenth and the nineteenth centuries, notes Alan Lester, we can discern the rise of a 'moral geography of the globe', where the Europeans felt responsible for 'distant strangers' (2000: 278). Thus, imperialism intersected with, fed into and drew from humanitarian ideologies and thought in *different* parts of the world/Empire. Subsequently, Lester et al.'s work focused on not 'national boundaries' (Britain's) but on 'transnational and trans-imperial connections' (2020: 2). They argue that 'the principles of freedom, civilisation and liberalism that motivated them were dissolved in a solution of violent racism through which British power was applied' in *various* colonies and geographical locations (2). Through a reading of three years—1838, 1857 and 1879—and the archive of Victorian imperialist statesmen and legal luminaries like James Stephen, Lester et al. demonstrate the linkage and common foundations (ideological, racism, etc.):

> [T]he ending of slavery and the rise of free trade doctrine, repeated Indian famines and the Uprising of 1857, the First and Second Afghan Wars, the First and Second Opium Wars, the Great Xhosa Cattle Killing and the Anglo-Zulu War, mass emigration from the British Isles, the self-governance of settler colonies in North America, Australasia and southern Africa and the devastation of Indigenous societies. (11)[5]

The Archive in 'New Imperial Histories'

The modes through which the archive has been read and employed have come in for criticism in the *new imperial history* turn. Nicholas Dirks summarises the problem with the slide between the production of the imperial archive and the production of the historical events within imperialism. Dirks writes:

> Begins the histories behind and beneath the production of the kinds of primary sources that have represented colonial knowledge even as they have been used to determine and justify colonial policy. The archive has enshrined, in [Michel] Foucault's sense, this raw material

[5] Philippa Levine and John Marriott in their Introduction to the massive *The Ashgate Research Companion to Modern Imperial Histories* (2012) argue that for many commentators, such as C.A. Bayly, 'modernity' in Europe itself is a consequence of its imperial actions—'The putative simultaneity of Europe's imperial ascent, globalisation and the birth of the modern world has led many to see an intimate interconnectedness.' (2)

However the trouble with this reading is, they note, 'that not only did Europe (or the west if we include the Americas) continue to display significant characteristics that might be regarded as pre-modern, but many of the features identified as modern were to be found equally in societies beyond and often unconnected to Europe.' (2)

> for subsequent historical representation. In the Indian case, the archive is both the precipitate of the history of conquest and rule and the basis on which that history has been written by colonial administrators. (2010: 95)

This 'colonial history' most notably in the 'Cambridge School' of historians, argues Dirks reading the archive of John Seeley and others, was in fact 'colonial fiction', which forwarded the idea that 'Indian politics emerged as a direct reflex of administrative initiatives set in motion by colonial rule' (95). Dirks continues:

> [such colonial histories argued] that local elites, the very groups that had been the collaborators for British rule, turned nationalist—in the context of participation in the progressively enlarged electoral arenas of provincial and municipal politics—when they realized that more of the pie could be obtained through autonomous political institutions than through colonial ones.... (95)

This meant

> [The Cambridge School] proved its arguments by using colonial sources—frequently police records and confidential files—that documented the spurious activities of nationalist figures in what was a large-scale colonial effort to track, contain, and debunk the very politics that sought to overthrow colonial rule. (96)

More recent readings have shown how colonial and imperial legacies and their discursive remains, even in the postcolonial era, turn to and retain its ideologies and representational modes. Nadine Attewell writes in *Better Britons*:

> [in] the afterlife of empire insofar as the projects of nation building with which it is concerned ... sexual reproduction [is the] key to, and a potent figure for, the (re)constitution of the national body after the 'end' of empire. (2014: 6)

This implies that the archive and the historical record—even as we debate what counts as the historical record—is very much an active constituent of the present postcolonial thought and actions as well.

*

The volumes here are only a small sample of the imperial archive. The range and depth of the archive are impossible to encapsulate in a few volumes. While I have made attempts elsewhere to capture some of this variety (Nayar 2007; 2009; 2013; 2016 [*Siege and Prison Writings*]; 2017; 2019), much more is required and possible. For example, the visual archive of the Empire, with its modalities and aesthetic grammars of 'composing' the subcontinent, whether in photography or painting (some of which may be found in Archer 1972), requires much more presence in the form of collections.

The present volumes focus on select aspects of the imperial archive: the accounts of 'discovery' and exploration—flora and fauna, geography, climate—the people of the subcontinent, English domesticity and social life in the subcontinent, the wars and skirmishes—including the *Mutiny* of 1857–1858—and the *civilisational mission.* It excludes legal documents and the many Acts and laws enacted by the British government.

Volume I consists of documents that deal with England's *discovery* of India, its exploration and mapping of the Indian land. This volume includes material as diverse as the letter from India of Thomas Stephens, often called 'the first Englishman in India', chorographic and cartographic accounts from geographical, meteorological, archaeological surveys that the various organisations and societies established for the purpose produced.

Volume II includes English studies of Indian languages and the social order. Ethnographic surveys of the subcontinent's people and cultural practices were published from the late eighteenth century. Practices like female infanticide, sati and thugee, seen as emblematic of the 'barbarous' Oriental, received special attention in the documentation. The characteristics of various tribes and ethnic group were also mapped in considerable detail.

Volume III shifts the focus entirely to the English home and social life. The documents include advice on gardening—an integral part of the English home—and on housekeeping. In the latter, the English were given instructions on how to monitor the domestic economy and manage the servants. Advice manuals on hunting and field sports were also published. Given the interracial dynamics at work, officers were issued manuals on etiquette and behaviour. Accounts of hill-stations and camps, and the social life in the Presidencies make up the rest of the volume.

Volume IV is a collection of accounts of a very different British life in India: as prisoners, under siege and in conditions of war. Starting with the notorious *Black Hole* of Calcutta to the 1857 *Mutiny*, the English wrote about being assailed, besieged and tormented in their war journals and prison accounts. These documented physical and emotional suffering, the losses of families and lives, even as they strove to depict British grit and determination.

Volume V documents England's *civilisational mission*. These documents offer a glimpse into British opinions and strategies on diverse subjects. It includes Macaulay's (in)famous Minute of 1835, accounts of medical missionary activities, views on establishing missionary activities and the British views on women's education.

Works Cited

Archer, Mildred. *Company Drawings in the India Office Library*. London: HMSO, 1972.

Attewell, Nadine. *Better Britons: Reproduction, National Identity, and the Afterlife of Empire*. Toronto: University of Toronto Press, 2014.

Auer, Blain. 'Early Modern Persian, Urdu, and English Historiography and the Imagination of Islamic India under British Rule', *Études de Lettres* 2–3 (2014): 199–206.

Bayly, C.A. *Empire and Information: Intelligence-Gathering and Social Communication in India*. Cambridge: Cambridge University Press, 1999.

Benton, A.H. *Indian Moral Instruction and Caste Problems: Solutions*. London: Longmans, Green and Co., 1917.

Burton, Antoinette and Isabel Hofmeyr. 'Introduction. The Spine of Empire? Books and the Making of an Imperial Commons'. In *Ten Books that Shaped the British Empire: Creating an Imperial Commons*, edited by Antoinette Burton and Isabel Hofmeyr. Durham and London: Duke University Press, 2014.

Burton, Antoinette. *Empire in Question: Reading, Writing, and Teaching British Imperialism*. Durham and London: Duke University Press, 2011.

Chaudhury, Zahid R. *Afterimage of Empire: Photography in Nineteenth-Century India*. Minneapolis: University of Minnesota Press, 2012.

Cohn, Bernard S. *Colonialism and Its Forms of Knowledge: The British in India*. New Delhi: Oxford University Press, 1997.

Damodaran, Vinita, Anna Winterbottom and Alan Lester, eds. *The East India Company and the Natural World*. London: Palgrave Macmillan, 2015.

Darwin, John. *The Empire Project: The Rise and Fall of the British World-System, 1830–1970*. Cambridge: Cambridge University Press, 2009.

Davis, Richard. 'Wilkins, Kasinatha, Hastings, and the First English *Bhagavad Gītā*', *International Journal of Hindu Studies* 19, no. 1–2 (2015): 39–57.

De Silva, Prasannajit. 'Representing Home Life Abroad: British Domestic Life in Early Nineteenth-Century India', *Visual Culture in Britain* 12, no. 3 (2011): 313–331.

Dirks, Nicholas B. 'Coda: The Burden of the Past.' In *The New Imperial Histories Reader*, edited by Stephen Howe, 92–105. Oxford: Routledge, 2010.

Dohman, Renata, ed. *Empire and Art: British India*. Manchester, UK: Manchester University Press, 2017.

Eaton, Natasha. *Colour, Art and Empire: Visual Culture and the Nomadism of Representation*. London: I.B. Tauris, 2013.

Edney, Matthew. *Mapping an Empire: The Geographical Construction of British India, 1753–1843*. Chicago: University of Chicago Press, 1997.

El Edroos, Aboobaker. *Modern Indian Etiquette: Of Mixed Society, Describing Ancient Social Usages and Important Indian Manners and Customs, Aiming at Social Amity Between Indians and Non-Indians*. Surat: H.R. Scott at the Mission Press, 1922.

Guégan, Xavier. 'Visualizing Alienation: Symbolism and Duality in Samuel Bourne's Photographs of British India', *Visual Culture in Britain* 12 no. 3 (2011): 349–365.

Hall, Catherine. *Civilising Subjects: Colony and Metropole in the English Imagination, 1830–1867*. Chicago: University of Chicago Press, 2002.

Joshi, Priya. *In Another Country: Colonialism, Culture, and the English Novel in India*. Oxford: Oxford University Press, 2003.

Leask, Nigel. *British Romantic Writers and the East: Anxieties of Empire*. Cambridge: Cambridge University Press, 1993.

Lelyveld, David. 'The Fate of Hindustani: Colonial Knowledge and the Project of a National Language'. In *Orientalism and the Postcolonial Predicament: Perspectives on South Asia*, edited by Carol Breckenridge and Peter van der Veer, 189–214. Philadelphia: University of Pennsylvania Press, 1993.

Lester, Alan, Kate Boehme and Peter Mitchell. *Ruling the World: Freedom, Civilisation and Liberalism in the Nineteenth-Century British Empire*. Cambridge: Cambridge University Press, 2021.

Lester, Alan. 'Obtaining the "due observance of justice": The geographies of colonial humanitarianism', *Environment and Planning D Society and Space* 20, no. 3 (2000): 277–293.

Levine, Philippa and John Marriott, eds. *The Ashgate Research Companion to Modern Imperial Histories*. London: Ashgate, 2016.

Macfie, Alexander Lyon. 'Thuggee: An Orientalist Construction?' *Rethinking History* 12, no. 3 (2008): 383–397.

Magee, Gary and Andrew Thompson. *Empire and Globalisation: Networks of People, Goods and Capital in the British World, c. 1850–1914*. Cambridge: Cambridge University Press, 2010.

Mahmood, Syed. *History of English Education in India, Its Rise, Development, Progress, Present Condition and Prospects. Being a Narrative of the Various Phases of Educational Policy and Measures Adopted under the British Rule from Its Beginning to the Present Period (1781 to 1893)*. Aligarh: M.A-O. College, 1895.

Malcolm, John. 'Notes of Instructions to Assistants and Officers Acting under the Orders of Major-General Sir John Malcolm, GCB.' In *A Memoir of*

Central India: Including Malwa, and Adjoining Provinces, Vol. 2, edited by John Malcolm. London: Kingsbury, Parbury and Allen, 1823.

Mir, Farina. *The Social Space of Language: Vernacular Culture in British Colonial Punjab*. Berkeley: University of California Press, 2010.

Naregal, Veena. *Language Politics, Elites, and the Public Sphere: Western India under Colonialism*. New Delhi: Permanent Black, 2001.

Nayar, Pramod K. 'English Discourse and India'. *Oxford Bibliographies Online*. New York: Oxford University Press, 2021, https://www.oxfordbibliographies.com/view/document/obo-9780190221911/obo-9780190221911-0114.xml.

______. 'Civil Modernity: The Management of Manners and Polite Imperial Relations in India, 1880–1930', *South Asia: Journal of South Asian Studies* 39, no. 4 (2016): 740–757.

______. 'Moral Readership and Political Apprenticeship: Commentaries on English Education in India, 1875–1930'. In *The Edinburgh History of Reading. Vol. IV. Subversive Readers*, edited by Jonathan Rose, 138–161. UK: Edinburgh University Press, 2020.

______. *Colonial Education and India*, 5 vols. London: Routledge, 2019.

______. *Days of the Raj: Life and Leisure in British India*. New Delhi: Penguin, 2009.

______. *English Siege and Prison Writings: From the 'Black Hole' to the 'Mutiny'*. London: Routledge, 2016.

______. *Indian Travel Writing, 1830–1947*. 1830–1947, 5 vols.

______. *The Penguin 1857 Reader*. New Delhi: Penguin, 2007.

______. *Women in Colonial India: Historical Documents and Sources*, 5 vols. London: Routledge, 2013.

Ogborn, Miles. *Indian Ink: Script and Print in the Making of the English East India Company*. Chicago and London: Chicago University Press, 2007.

Orsini, Francesca. *The Hindi Public Sphere: Language and Literature in the Age of Nationalism*. Oxford: Oxford University Press, 2010.

Pinney, Christopher. 'Sepia Mutiny: Colonial Photography and Its Others in India.' In *Feeling Photography*, edited by Elspeth Brown and Thy Phu, 71–92. Durham, NC: Duke University Press, 2014.

Rao, Velcheru Narayana. 'Print and Prose: Pundits, *Karanams*, and the East India Company in the Making of Modern Telugu'. In *India's Literary History: Essays on the Nineteenth Century*, edited by Stuart Blackburn and Vasudha Dalmia, 146–166. New Delhi: Permanent Black, 2004.

Richards, Thomas. *The Imperial Archive: Knowledge and the Fantasy of Empire*. London: Verso, 1993.

Roy, Anindyo. *Civility and Empire: Literature and Culture in British India, 1822–1922*. London: Routledge, 2005.

Teltscher, Kate. *India Inscribed: European and English Writing on India, 1600–1800*. Delhi: Oxford University Press, 1997.

Tobin, Beth Fowkes. *Picturing Imperial Power: Colonial Subjects in Eighteenth-Century British Painting*. Durham, NC: Duke University Press, 1999, 110–138.

Trivedi, Harish. *Colonial Transactions: English Literature and India*. Calcutta: Papyrus, 1993.

Viswanathan, Gauri. *Masks of Conquest: English Literary Studies and India*. London: Faber & Faber, 1990.

Webb, William Trego. *English Etiquette for Indian Gentlemen*. 5th ed. 1895. Calcutta: S.K. Lahiri, 1915.

Williamson, Thomas. *Oriental Field Sports*. London: W. Bulmer, 1808.

INTRODUCTION

The British ascendancy in India did not proceed smoothly, and colonisation was always a militarised zone of interest, action and process.

The imperial archive holds numerous records, eyewitness accounts and newspaper reports on the wars fought, from the epochal Anglo-Mysore Wars to the disastrous Afghan campaigns. The 'Mutiny' of 1857 produced reams and reams of fiction, memoirs and accounts.

The British public 'back home' read heroic tales of their soldiers' valour, the 'treacherous' and 'cruel' natives who did not respect the norms of war, the suffering of the British, etc. When J.Z. Holwell recounted the sufferings of the English in the 'Black Hole' of Calcutta in his account, he was inaugurating a tradition of 'siege' writings. Works like that of James Bristow added to the corpus of such work. Recalling in detail the humid conditions inside the prison, Holwell claims heroic valour and compassion when drawing his self-portrait in describing this incident. Bristow ensures that we recognise the unbelievable cruelty of his tormentor, Tipu Sultan, who had imprisoned him. Inglis's account of the siege of Lucknow focuses simultaneously on the problems of domestic arrangements—children, food, hygiene—in the midst of the siege and the anxiety around the menfolk fighting off the Indian 'mutineers'.

Men and women 'out there' were the braves, battling insurmountable odds in the interest of the Empire. The archives enabled the making of entire myths and stereotypes, and these stayed as important factors in policymaking and imperial attitudes towards the colonised, especially after 1857. These documents revealed an entirely new subcontinent to the readers back in England. Many of the books and accounts of war in the subcontinent were reviewed, and newspapers like *The Times* had made it a point to carry news reports of the 'war in the East Indies' from the time of the Anglo-Mysore wars in the late eighteenth century.

ACKNOWLEDGEMENTS

The Raj has been a perennial favourite when it comes to research and writing, and I cannot remember a year when I did *not* do some 'Raj work'.

Chandra Sekhar of Bloomsbury was very receptive to the project idea, and has been incisive and encouraging when it came to subjects like the volumes' organisation, content and final form—to him, this project owes much.

I express my thanks to journals and anthologies, and their editors and reviewers whose comments have enabled me to sharpen my thoughts on the Raj-topic-of-the-moment. Among journals, I acknowledge: *South Asia, South Asian Review, Anglo-Saxonica* and *Asiatic*. Among the anthologies, I acknowledge *Ireland's Imperial Connections*; *The Edinburgh History of Reading*; *The English Renaissance, Orientalism, and the Idea of Asia*; *Cultural Histories of India*. To Debra Johanyak and Walter S. Lim, Rita Banerjee, Daniel Roberts and Jonathan Wright, Mary Hammond and Jonathan Rose, editors of these fabulous anthologies, many thanks for your invitation to contribute and the work you put into the volumes of which I am now a part.

To Kate Teltscher, whose work *India Inscribed* showed me where to go way back in the mid-1990s, I owe an intellectual debt of enormous proportions.

I am also grateful to publishers and editors at Penguin, Bloomsbury, Palgrave-Macmillan, Edinburgh University Press, Orient BlackSwan, Wiley-Blackwell and Routledge for their comments, suggestions and, above all, interest in this area and my contributions to it.

To Soma Ghosh, Librarian (English) at the Salar Jung Museum, Hyderabad, and her constant efforts, all undertaken with cheer and grace, to obtain materials when I have worked there, immeasurable gratitude.

Many books germinate in conversations with Anna Kurian, who is always enthusiastic about any Raj-work I do, especially if they are multivolume projects. For the constant-traveller role that you assay with such commitment, solidarity and affection, it is my privilege, Anna, to acknowledge you.

Thank you, Molly ('Chechu'), for enquiring lovingly about her 'little one'.

Nandana Dutta has been unceasing in her interest in my work, and her always gentle and loving urging to think in certain ways, even as she tries to catch up with her reading of what I publish. To your attention, insights and perspicacity, Nandana—much, much gratitude.

Professor K. Narayana Chandran established, for some of us willing ones, the standards in academic scholarship and publishing—that he sustains these standards even now, after four decades, is nothing short of the marvellous. To KNC's indomitable spirit of inquiry and work ethic, and showing us the way to do things, I am very grateful.

Friends who drop in 'WhatsAppingly', regularly, to check on me—Neelu, Bhalla, Ajeet, Kulsoom, Om, Archana, Ashish, Krishna Ram, Sai Jawahar, Savita, Vaishali, Soma and Zahid—thank you.

To Nandini, Pranav, my parents and parents-in-law, I owe unquantifiable gratitude, for never complaining at the volume of work I take on, my frequently distracted state of being and, more importantly, for creating an extraordinarily supportive environment.

And thank you, Shubha, for obtaining, wizard-like, essays and journal articles in minutes, and for your enthusiasm for my work.

To the works of P.G. Wodehouse, Agatha Christie, Stephen King, the comics around Batman—my regular reading—many of which unwittingly capture the horror, the abyss and the comedy of academia, I can never express enough gratitude.

It is a pleasure to thank Atul Nair who compiled many of the materials meticulously.

I am grateful to the Institution of Eminence (IoE) project's Professional Development Fund.

J.Z. Holwell

***A Genuine Narrative of the Deplorable Deaths of the English Gentlemen and others who were suffocated in Fort-William, at Calcutta, in the Kingdom of Bengal, in the night succeeding the 20th day of June, 1756, in a letter to a friend*. London: Printed for A. Millar in the Strand, 1758.**

A GENUINE

NARRATIVE

OF THE

DEPLORABLE DEATHS

OF THE

ENGLISH GENTLEMEN, and Others, who were ſuffocated in the BLACK-HOLE in FORT-WILLIAM, at CALCUTTA, in the Kingdom of BENGAL; in the Night ſucceeding the 20th Day of JUNE, 1756.

In a LETTER to a FRIEND,

By J. Z. HOLWELL, Eſq;

——— —— *Quæque ipſe miſerrima vidi,*
Et quarum pars magna fui. Quis talia fando,
Myrmidonum, Dolopumve, aut duri miles Ulyſſei
Temperet a lachrymis? Virg. Æneid. Lib. ii.

LONDON:
Printed for A. MILLAR in the STRAND.
MDCCLVIII.
(Price One Shilling.)

TO THE READER.

THE following narrative will appear, upon perufal, to be a fimple detail of a moft melancholy event, delivered in the genuine language of fincere concern, in a letter to a friend; from whom the greateft kindneffes had been received, and in whom the greateft confidence was placed. It was written on board the veffel in which the author returned from the Eaft-Indies, when he had leifure to reflect, and was at liberty to throw upon paper, what was too ftrongly impreſſed upon his memory, ever to wear out. If therefore it appears in ſome places, a little paſſionate; in others, ſomewhat diffuſe; and through the whole, tinctured with that diſpoſition under which it was written; the occaſion, and the nature of the performance, will ſufficiently excuſe what might have been conſidered as imperfections, if it had been intended for the public view; and which may perhaps be conſidered in another light, now, that through a train of unforeſeen accidents, it comes to appear in print.

The ſubject being of a very mixed nature, and ſomething more than a bare relation of private calamity, rendered many people curious to ſee it, when it was once known, that ſuch a paper exiſted; and as there was nothing contained in it, that required either much ſecrecy, or circumſpection; it has been freely communicated to ſeveral, and amongſt thoſe, to ſome perſons of the firſt diſtinction; who thought it might gratify public expectation, more eſpecially if it appeared in the ſame natural, and undiſguiſed dreſs, in which they had ſeen it; for truth, and more eſpecially ſo affecting a truth, ſtands little in need of ornament, and appears to more advantage, the leſs it is aſſiſted by the arts of writing, to which the author being a ſtranger, he truſted to his feeling, and endeavoured to expreſs by his pen, the emotions of his heart. He the more readily yielded to this requeſt of his friends, from the following motives, which as they wrought much upon him, may poſſibly have ſome weight with you.

It is ſomewhat rare, to find tranſactions of an extraordinary nature, delivered circumſtantially by thoſe who are not only acquainted with, but were alſo actors in them; whilſt the matter is freſh in their minds, and conſequently when they are fitteſt, to give a clear, connected, and impartial account. This therefore having been his original intention, though for the ſatisfaction only of a private friend; yet when called upon to make it public, it appeared to him a very persuasive argument, as he was conscious to himself, that he had written it with the strictest regard to veracity, in every point, and to disburthen his thoughts of that load of affliction, which would have been as intolerable as the misfortune itself, if both had not been qualified by the remembrance of that mercy by which he was delivered, and which seemed to claim a grateful return of public acknowledgement, for so peculiar a deliverance.

He was farther moved, by the consideration that there are some scenes in real life, so full of misery and horror, that the boldest imagination would not dare to feign them, for fear of shocking credibility. He thought ſuch ſcenes as theſe could not be permitted, by a wiſe, a beneficent being, but for the ſake of their becoming leſſons to mankind ; and he therefore thought, that this intention could never be better anſwered, than by conſenting to render them public ; that by this means, a door of hope, and of confidence may be opened, to ſuch as may hereafter, fall under like tryals, by giving them an inſtance (and ſure a ſtronger cannot well be given) that we ought never to deſpair, when innocence and duty have been the cauſes of our diſtreſs.

A LETTER FROM J. Z. HOLWELL, Esq; TO Wm. DAVIS, Esq;

From on board the SYREN-SLOOP, the 28th of February, 1757.

DEAR SIR,

THE confusion which the late capture of the East-India company's settlements in Bengal must necessarily excite in the city of London, will, I fear be not a little heightened by the miserable deaths of the greatest part of those gentlemen, who were reduced to the sad necessity of surrendering themselves prisoners at discretion in Fort William.

By narratives made public you will only know, that of one hundred and forty-ſix prisoners, one hundred and twenty-three were ſmothered in the Black-Hole priſon, in the night of the 20th of June, 1756. Few ſurvived capable of giving any detail of the manner in which it happened; and of theſe I believe none have attempted it: for my own part, I have often ſet down with this reſolution, and as often relinquiſhed the melancholy taſk, not only from the diſturbance and affliction it raiſed a-freſh in my remembrance, but from the conſideration of the impoſſibility of finding language capable of raiſing an adequate idea of the horrors of the ſcene I eſſayed to draw. But as I believe the annals of the world cannot produce an incident like it in any degree or proportion to all the diſmal circumſtances attending it, and as my own health of body and peace of mind are once again, in a great meaſure, recovered from the injuries they ſuffered from that fatal night, I cannot allow it to be buried in oblivion; though ſtill conſcious, that however high the colouring my retentive memory may ſupply, it will fall infinitely ſhort of the horrors accompanying this ſcene. Theſe defects muſt, and I doubt not, will be aſſiſted by your own humane and benevolent imagination; in the exerciſe of which I never knew you deficient, where unmerited diſtreſs was the object.

The ſea-air has already had that ſalutary effect on my conſtitution I expected; and my mind enjoys a calm it has been many months a ſtranger to, ſtrengthened by a clear chearful ſky and atmoſphere, joined to an unuſual pleaſant gale, with which we are paſſing the equinoctial. I can now, therefore, look back with leſs agitation on the dreadful night I am going to deſcribe; and with a grateful heart ſincerely acknowledge, and deeply revere that Providence, which alone could have preſerved me through that and all my ſucceeding ſufferings and hazards.

Before I conduct you into the Black-Hole, it is necessary you should be acquainted with a few introductory circumstances. The Suba ‡ and his troops were in possession of the fort before six in the evening. I had in all three interviews: the last in Durbar || before seven, when he repeated his assurances to me, *on the word of a soldier*, that no harm should come to us; and indeed I believe his orders were only general. That we should for that night be secured; and that what followed was the result of revenge and resentment in the breasts of the lower Jemmaatdaars †, to whose custody we were delivered, for the number of their order killed during the siege. Be this as it may, as soon as it was dark, we were all, without distinction, directed by the guard over us, to collect ourselves into one body, and sit down quietly under the arched Veranda or piazza, to the

‡ Suzajud-Dowla, viceroy of Bengal, Bakar, and Orixa. || In council. † An officer of the rank of Serjeant.

weſt of the Black-Hole priſon, and the barracks to the left of the court of guard; and juſt over againſt the windows of the governor's eaſterly apartments. Beſides the guard over us, another was placed at the foot of the ſtairs at the ſouth end of this Veranda, leading up to the ſouth-eaſt baſtion, to prevent any of us eſcaping that way. On the parade (where you will remember the two twenty-four pounders ſtood) were alſo drawn up about four or five hundred gun-men with lighted matches.

At this time the factory was in flames to the right and left of us; to the right the Armory and Laboratory; to the left the Carpenters' yard: though at this time we imagined it was the Cotta-ware-houſes ‡. Various were our conjectures on this appearance; the fire advanced with rapidity on both ſides; and it was the prevailing opinion, that they intended ſuffocating us between the two fires: and this notion was confirmed by

‡ The company's cloth warehouſes.

the appearance, about half an hour paſt ſeven, of ſome officers and people with lighted torches in their hands, who went into all the apartments under the eaſterly curtain to the right of us; to which we apprehended they were ſetting fire, to expedite their ſcheme of burning us. On this we preſently came to a reſolution, of ruſhing on the guard, ſeizing their ſcymitars, and attacking the troops upon the parade, rather than be thus tamely roaſted to death. But to be ſatisfied of their intentions, I advanced, at the requeſt of Meſſrs. Baillie, Jenks, and Revely, to ſee if they were really ſetting fire to the apartments, and found the contrary; for in fact, as it appeared afterwards, they were only ſearching for a place to confine us in; the laſt they examined being the barracks of the court of guard behind us.

Here I muſt detain you a little, to do honour to the memory of a man, to whom I had in many inſtances been a friend, and who, on this occaſion, demonſtrated his ſenſibility of it in a degree worthy of a much higher rank. His name was Leech, the company's ſmith, as well as clerk of the pariſh; this man had made his eſcape when the Moors entered the fort, and returned juſt as it was dark, to tell me he had provided a boat, and would enſure my eſcape, if I would follow him through a paſſage few were acquainted with, and by which he had then entered. (This might eaſily have been accompliſhed, as the guard put over us took but very ſlight notice of us.) I thanked him in the beſt terms I was able; but told him it was a ſtep I could not prevail on myſelf to take, as I ſhould thereby very ill repay the attachment the gentlemen and the garriſon had ſhewn to me; and, that I was reſolved to ſhare their fate, be it what it would: but preſſed him to ſecure his own eſcape without loſs of time; to which he gallantly replied, that "then he was reſolved to ſhare mine, and would not leave me."

To myſelf and the world I ſhould ſurely have ſtood excuſed in embracing the overture abovementioned, could I have conceived what immediately followed; for I had ſcarce time to make him an anſwer, before we obſerved part of the guard drawn up on the parade, advance to us with the officers who had been viewing the rooms. They ordered us all to riſe and go into the barracks to the left of the court of guard. The barracks, you may remember, have a large wooden platform for the ſoldiers to ſleep on, and are open to the weſt by arches and a ſmall parapet-wall, correſponding to the arches of the Veranda without. In we went moſt readily, and were pleaſing ourſelves with the proſpect of paſſing a comfortable night on the platform, little dreaming of the infernal apartment in reſerve for us. For we were no ſooner all within the barracks, than the guard advanced to the inner arches and parapet-wall; and, with their muſkets preſented, ordered us to go into the room at the ſouthermoſt end of the barracks, commonly called the Black-Hole priſon; whilſt others from the Court of Guard, with clubs and drawn ſcymitars, preſſed upon thoſe of us next to them. This ſtroke was ſo ſudden, ſo unexpected, and the throng and preſſure ſo great upon us next the door of the Black-Hole priſon, there was no reſiſting it; but like one agitated wave impelling another, we were oblig-ed to give way and enter; the reſt fol-lowed like a torrent, few amongſt us, the ſoldiers excepted, having the leaſt idea of the dimenſions or nature of a place we had never ſeen: for if we had, we ſhould at all events have ruſhed upon the guard, and been, as the leſſer evil, by our own choice cut to pieces.

Amongſt the firſt that entered, were myſelf, Meſſieurs Baillie, Jenks, Cooke, T. Coles, Enſign Scot, Revely, Law, Buchanan, &c. I got poſſeſſion of the window neareſt the door, and took Meſ-ſieurs Coles and Scot into the window with me, they being both wounded (the firſt I believe mortally). The reſt of the abovementioned gentlemen were cloſe round about me. It was now about eight o'clock.

Figure to yourſelf, my friend, if poſſible, the ſituation of a hundred and forty ſix wretches, exhauſted by continual fatigue and action, thus crammed together in a cube of about eighteen feet, in a cloſe ſultry night, in Bengal, ſhut up to the eaſtward and ſouthward (the only quarters from whence air could reach us) by dead walls, and by a wall and door to the north, open only to the weſtward by two windows, ſtrongly barred with iron, from which we could receive ſcarce any the leaſt circulation of freſh air.

What muſt enſue, appeared to me in lively and dreadful colours, the inſtant I caſt my eyes round and ſaw the ſize and ſituation of the room. Many unſucceſsful attempts were made to force the door; for having nothing but our hands to work with, and the door opening inward, all endeavours were vain and fruitleſs.

Obſerving every one giving way to the violence of paſſions, which I foreſaw muſt be fatal to them, I requeſted ſilence might be preſerved, whilſt I ſpoke to them, and in the moſt pathetic and moving terms, which occurred, "I begg'd and intreated, that as they had paid a ready obedience to me in the day, they would now for their own ſakes and the ſakes of thoſe, who were dear to them, and were intereſted in the preſervation of their lives, regard the advice I had to give them. I aſſured them, the return of day would give us air and liberty; urged to them, that the only chance we had left for ſuſtaining this misfortune, and ſurviving the night, was the preſerving a calm mind and quiet reſignation to our fate; intreating them to curb, as much as poſſible, every agitation of mind and body, as raving and giving a looſe to their paſſions could anſwer no purpoſe, but that of haſtening their deſtruction."

This remonſtrance produced a ſhort interval of peace, and gave me a few minutes for reflection: though even this pauſe was not a little diſturbed by the cries and groans of the many wounded, and more particularly of my two companions in the window. Death, attended with the moſt cruel train of circumſtances, I plainly perceived muſt prove our inevitable deſtiny: I had ſeen this common migration in too many ſhapes, and accuſtomed myſelf to think on the ſubject with too much propriety to be alarmed at the proſpect, and indeed felt much more for my wretched companions than myſelf.

Amongſt the guards poſted at the windows, I obſerved an old Jemmautdaar near me, who ſeemed to carry ſome compaſſion for us in his countenance; and indeed he was the only one of the many in his ſtation, who diſcovered the leaſt trace of humanity. I called him to me, and in the moſt perſuaſive terms I was capable, urged him to commiſerate the ſufferings he was a witneſs to, and preſſed him to endeavour to get us ſeparated, half in one place, and half in another; and that he ſhould in the morning receive a thouſand Rupees for this act of tenderneſs. He promiſed he would attempt it, and withdrew; but in a few minutes returned, and told me it was impoſſible. I then thought I had been deficient in my offer, and promiſed him two thouſand: He withdrew a ſecond time, but returned ſoon, and (with I believe much real pity and concern) told me, it was not practicable; that it could not be done but by the Suba's order, and that no one dared awake him.

During this interval, though their paſſions were leſs violent, their uneaſineſs encreaſed. We had been but few minutes confined before every one fell into a perſpiration ſo profuſe, you can form no idea of it. This conſequently brought on a raging thirſt, which ſtill increaſed, in proportion as the body was drained of its moiſture.

Various expedients were thought of to give more room and air. To obtain the former, it was moved to put off their cloaths: This was approved, as a happy motion, and in a few minutes I believe every man was ſtripped (myſelf, Mr. Court, and the two wounded young gentlemen by me excepted) for a little time they flattered themſelves with having gained a mighty advantage; every hat was put in motion to produce a circulation of air, and Mr. Baillie propoſed that every man ſhould ſit down on his hams: as they were truly in the ſituation of drowning wretches, no wonder they caught at every thing that bore a flattering appearance of ſaving them. This expedient was ſeveral times put in practice, and at each time many of the poor creatures, whoſe natural ſtrength was leſs than others, or had been more exhauſted and could not immediately recover their legs, as others did when the word was given to RISE, fell to riſe no more: for they were inſtantly trod to death, or ſuffocated. When the whole body ſat down, they were ſo cloſely wedged together, that they were oblig-ed to uſe many efforts, before they could put themſelves in motion to get up again.

Before nine o'clock every man's thirſt grew intolerable, and reſpiration diffi-cult. Our ſituation was much more wretched than that of ſo many miſer-able animals in an exhauſted receiver; no circulation of freſh air ſufficient to continue life, nor yet enough diveſted of its vivifying particles to put a ſpeedy period to it.

Efforts were again made to force the door, but in vain. Many inſults were uſed to the guard to provoke them to fire in upon us (which as I learned af-terwards, were carried to much greater lengths, when I was no more ſenſible of what was tranſacted). For my own part, I hitherto felt little pain or uneaſineſs, but what reſulted from my anxiety for the ſufferings of thoſe within. By keeping my face between two of the bars, I obtained air enough to give my lungs eaſy play, though my perſpiration was exceſſive, and thirſt commencing. At this period, ſo ſtrong a urinous volatile effluvia came from the priſon, that I was not able to turn my head that way, for more than a few ſeconds at a time.

Now every body, excepting thoſe ſituated in and near the windows, began to grow outrageous, and many dilirious: "WATER, WATER," became the general cry. And the old Jemmautdaar, beforementioned, taking pity on us, ordered the people to bring ſome ſkins of water, little dreaming, I believe, of its fatal effects. This was what I dreaded. I foreſaw it would prove the ruin of the ſmall chance left us, and eſſayed many times to ſpeak to him privately to forbid its being brought; but the clamour was ſo loud, it became impoſſible. The water appeared. Words cannot paint to you the universal agitation and raving the sight of it threw us into. I had flattered myself that some, by preserving an equal temper of mind, might outlive the night; but now the reflection, which gave me the greatest pain, was, that I saw no possibility of one escaping to tell the dismal tale.

Until the water came, I had myself not suffered much from thirst, which instantly grew excessive. We had no means of conveying it into the prison, but by hats forced through the bars; and thus myself and Messieurs Coales and Scot (notwithstanding the pains they suffered from their wounds) supplied them as fast as possible. But those, who have experienced intense thirst, or are acquainted with the cause and nature of this appetite, will be sufficiently sensible it could receive no more than a momentary alleviation; the cause still subsisted. Though we brought full hats within the bars, there ensued such violent struggles, and frequent contests to get at it, that before it reached the lips of any one, there would be ſcarcely a ſmall tea-cup full left in them. Theſe ſupplies, like ſprinkling water on fire, only ſerved to feed and raiſe the flame.

Oh! my dear Sir, how ſhall I give you a conception of what I felt at the cries and ravings of thoſe in the remoter parts of the priſon, who could not entertain a probable hope of obtaining a drop, yet could not diveſt themſelves of expectation, however unavailing! And others calling on me by the tender conſiderations of friendſhip and affection, and who knew they were really dear to me. Think, if poſſible, what my heart muſt have ſuffered at ſeeing and hearing their diſtreſs, without having it in my power to relieve them: For the confuſion now became general and horrid. Several quitted the other window (the only chance they had for life) to force their way to the water, and the throng and preſs upon the window was beyond bearing; many forcing their paſſage from the further part of the room, preſſed down thoſe in their way, who had leſs ſtrength, and trampled them to death.

Can it gain belief, that this ſcene of miſery proved entertainment to the brutal wretches without? But ſo it was; and they took care to keep us ſupplied with water, that they might have the ſatisfaction of ſeeing us fight for it, as they phraſed it, and held up lights to the bars, that they might loſe no part of the inhuman diverſion.

From about nine to near eleven, I ſuſtained this cruel ſcene and painful ſituation, ſtill ſupplying them with water, though my legs were almoſt broke with the weight againſt them. By this time I myſelf was very near preſſed to death, and my two companions, with Mr. William Parker (who had forced himſelf into the window) were *really* ſo.

For a great while they preſerved a reſpect and regard to me, more than indeed I could well expect, our circumſtances conſidered; but now all diſtinction was loſt. My friend Baillie, Meſſrs. Jenks, Revely, Law, Buchanan, Simſon, and ſeveral others, for whom I had a real eſteem and affection, had for ſome time been dead at my feet; and were now trampled upon by every corporal or common ſoldier, who, by the help of more robuſt conſtitutions, had forced their way to the window, and held faſt by the bars over me, till at laſt I became ſo preſſed and wedged up, I was deprived of all motion.

Determined now to give every thing up, I called to them, and begged, as the laſt inſtance of their regard, they would remove the preſſure upon me, and permit me to retire out of the window, to die in quiet. They gave way; and with much difficulty I forced a paſſage into the center of the priſon, where the throng was leſs by the many dead, (then I believe amounting to one-third) and the numbers who flocked to the windows: for by this time they had water alſo at the other window.

In the Black-Hole there is a platform * corresponding with that in the barracks: I travelled over the dead, and repaired to the further end of it, just opposite the other window, and seated myself on the platform between Mr. Dumbleton and captain Stevenson; the former just then expiring. I was still happy in the same calmness of mind I had preserved the whole time; death I expected as unavoidable, and only lamented its slow approach, tho' the moment I quitted the window my breathing grew short and painful.

Here my poor friend Mr. Edward Eyre came staggering over the dead to me, and with his usual coolness and good nature, asked me how I did? but fell and expired before I had time to make him a reply. I laid myself down on some of the dead behind me, on the platform; and, recommending myself

* This platform was raised between three and four feet from the floor, open underneath; it extended the whole length of the east side of the prison, and was above six feet wide.

to heaven, had the comfort of thinking my ſufferings could have no long duration.

My thirſt grew now inſupportable, and difficulty of breathing much increaſed; and had not remained in this ſituation, I believe, ten minutes, when I was ſeized with a pain in my breaſt, and palpitation of my heart, both to the moſt exquiſite degree. Theſe rouſed and obliged me to get up again; but ſtill the pain, palpitation, thirſt, and difficulty of breathing increaſed. I retained my ſenſes notwithſtanding, and had the grief to ſee death not ſo near me as I hoped; but could no longer bear the pains I ſuffered without attempting a relief, which I knew freſh air would and could only give me. I inſtantly determined to puſh for the window oppoſite to me; and by an effort of double the ſtrength I ever before poſſeſſed, gained the third rank at it, with one hand ſeized a bar, and by that means gained the ſecond, though I think there were at leaſt ſix or ſeven ranks between me and the window.

In a few moments my pain, palpitation, and difficulty of breathing ceaſed; but my thirſt continued intolerable. I called aloud for "WATER FOR GOD'S SAKE:" had been concluded dead; but as ſoon as they heard me amongſt them, they had ſtill the reſpect and tenderneſs for me, to cry out, "GIVE HIM WATER, GIVE HIM WATER!" nor would one of them at the window attempt to touch it until I had drank. But from the water I found no relief; my thirſt was rather increaſed by it; ſo I determined to drink no more, but patiently wait the event; and kept my mouth moiſt from time to time by ſucking the perſpiration out of my ſhirt-ſleeves, and catching the drops as they fell, like heavy rain from my head and face: you can hardly imagine how unhappy I was if any of them eſcaped my mouth.

I came into the priſon without coat or waiſtcoat; the ſeaſon was too hot to bear the former, and the latter tempted the avarice of one of the guards, who robbed me of it when we were under the Veranda. Whilſt I was at this ſecond window, I was obſerved by one of my miſerable companions on the right of me, in the expedient of allaying my thirſt by ſucking my ſhirt-ſleeve. He took the hint, and robbed me from time to time of a conſiderable part of my ſtore; though after I detected him, I had ever the addreſs to begin on that ſleeve firſt, when I thought my reſervoirs were ſufficiently repleniſhed; and our mouths and noſes often met in the conteſt. This plunderer I found afterwards was a worthy young gentleman in the ſervice, Mr. Luſhington, one of the few who eſcaped from death, and ſince paid me the compliment of aſſuring me, he believed he owed his life to the many comfortable draughts he had from my ſleeves. I mention this incident, as I think nothing can give you a more lively idea of the melancholy ſtate and diſtreſs we were reduced to. Before I hit upon this happy expedient, I had, in an ungovernable fit of thirſt, attempted drinking my urine; but it was ſo intenſely bitter there was no enduring a ſecond taſte, whereas no Briſtol water could be more ſoft or pleaſant than what aroſe from perſpiration.

By half an hour paſt eleven the much greater number of thoſe living were in an outrageous delirium, and the others quite ungovernable; few retaining any calmneſs, but the ranks next the windows. By what I had felt myſelf, I was fully ſenſible what thoſe within ſuffered; but had only pity to beſtow upon them, not then thinking how ſoon I ſhould myſelf become a greater object of it.

They all now found, that water, inſtead of relieving, rather heightened their uneaſineſſes; and, "AIR, AIR," was the general cry. Every inſult that could be deviſed againſt the guard, all the opprobrious names and abuſe that the Suba, Monickchund &c, * could be

* Rajah Monickchund, appointed by the Suba governor of Calcutta.

loaded with, were repeated to provoke the guard to fire upon us, every man that could, rushing tumultuously towards the windows with eager hopes of meeting the first shot. Then a general prayer to heaven, to hasten the approach of the flames to the right and left of us, and put a period to our misery. But these failing, they whose strength and spirits were quite exhausted, laid themselves down and expired quietly upon their fellows: others who had yet some strength and vigour left, made a last effort for the windows, and several succeeded by leaping and scrambling over the backs and heads of those in the first ranks; and got hold of the bars, from which there was no removing them. Many to the right and left sunk with the violent pressure, and were soon suffocated; for a now a steam arose from the living and the dead, which affected us in all its circumstances, as if we were forcibly held with our heads over a bowl full of strong volatile spirit of hartshorn, until ſuffocated; nor could the effluvia of the one be diſtinguiſhed from the other, and frequently, when I was forced by the load upon my head and ſhoulders, to hold my face down, I was obliged, near as I was to the window, inſtantly to raiſe it again to eſcape ſuffocation.

I need not, my dear friend, ask your commiſeration, when I tell you, that in this plight, from half an hour paſt eleven till near two in the morning, I ſuſtained the weight of a heavy man, with his knees in my back, and the preſſure of his whole body on my head. A Dutch ſerjeant, who had taken his ſeat upon my left ſhoulder, and a Topaz * bearing on my right; all which nothing could have enabled me long to ſupport, but the props and preſſure equally ſuſtaining me all around. The two latter I frequently diſlodged, by ſhifting my hold on the bars, and driving my knuckles into their ribs; but my friend above

* A black Chriſtian ſoldier: uſually termed ſubjects of Portugal.

ſtuck faſt, and as he held by two bars, was immoveable.

When I had bore this conflict above an hour, with a train of wretched reflections, and ſeeing no glimpſe of hope on which to found a proſpect of relief, my ſpirits, reſolution, and every ſentiment of religion gave way. I found I was unable much longer to ſupport this trial, and could not bear the dreadful thoughts of retiring into the inner part of the priſon, where I had before ſuffered ſo much. Some infernal ſpirit, taking the advantage of this period, brought to my remembrance my having a ſmall claſp penknife in my pocket, with which I determined inſtantly to open my arteries, and finiſh a ſyſtem no longer to be born. I had got it out, when heaven interpoſed and reſtored me to freſh ſpirits and reſolution, with an abhorrence of the act of cowardice I was juſt going to commit: I exerted a-new my ſtrength and fortitude; but the repeated trials and efforts I made to diſlodge the inſufferable incumbrances upon me at laſt quite exhauſted me, and towards two o'clock, finding I muſt quit the window, or ſink where I was, I reſolved on the former, having bore, truly for the ſake of others, infinitely more for life than the beſt of it is worth.

In the rank cloſe behind me was an officer of one of the ſhips, whoſe name was Carey, and who had behaved with much bravery during the ſiege, (his wife, a fine woman tho' country-born, would not quit him, but accompanied him into the priſon, and was one who ſurvived.) This poor wretch had been long raving for water and air; I told him I was determined to give up life, and recommended his gaining my ſtation. On my quitting, he made a fruitleſs attempt to get my place; but the Dutch ſerjeant who ſat on my ſhoulder ſupplanted him.

Poor Carey expreſſed his thankfulneſs, and ſaid, he would give up life too; but it was with the utmoſt labour we forced our way from the window, (ſeveral in the inner ranks appearing to me dead ſtanding *.) He laid himſelf down to die: and his death, I believe, was very ſudden; for he was a ſhort, full, ſanguine man: his ſtrength was great, and I imagine, had he not retired with me, I ſhould never have been able to have forced my way.

I was at this time ſenſible of no pain and little uneaſineſs: I can give you no better idea of my ſituation than by repeating my ſimile of the bowl of ſpirit of hartſhorn. I found a ſtupor coming on apace, and laid myſelf down by that gallant old man, the reverend Mr. Jervas Bellamy, who lay dead with his ſon the lieutenant, hand in hand, near the ſouthermoſt wall of the priſon.

When I had lain there ſome little time, I ſtill had reflection enough to ſuffer ſome uneaſineſs in the thought, that I ſhould be trampled upon, when dead, as I myſelf had done to others. With ſome difficulty I raiſed myſelf, and gained the platform a ſecond time, where I pre-

* Unable to fall by the throng and equal preſſure round.

ſently loſt all ſenſation: the laſt trace of ſenſibility that I have been able to recollect after my laying down, was my ſaſh being uneaſy about my waſte, which I untied and threw from me.

Of what paſſed in this interval to the time of my reſurrection from this hole of horrors, I can give you no account; and indeed, the particulars mentioned by ſome of the gentlemen who ſurvived, (ſolely by the number of thoſe dead, by which they gained a freer acceſſion of air, and approach to the windows) were ſo exceſſively abſurd and contradictory, as to convince me, very few of them retained their ſenſes; or at leaſt, loſt them ſoon after they came into the open air, by the fever they carried out with them.

In my own eſcape from abſolute death the hand of heaven was manifeſtly exerted: the manner take as follows. When the day broke, and the gentlemen found that no intreaties could prevail to get the door opened, it occurred to one of them, (I think to Mr. ſecretary Cooke) to make a ſearch for me, in hopes I might have influence enough to gain a releaſe from this ſcene of miſery. Accordingly Meſſrs. Luſhington and Walcot undertook the ſearch, and by my ſhirt diſcovered me under the dead upon the platform. They took me from thence; and imagining I had ſome ſigns of life, brought me towards the window I had firſt poſſeſſion of.

But as life was equally dear to every man, (and the ſtench ariſing from the dead bodies was grown intolerable) no one would give up his ſtation in or near the window: ſo they were obliged to carry me back again. But ſoon after captain Mills (now captain of the company's yatcht) who was in poſſeſſion of a ſeat in the window, had the humanity to offer to reſign it. I was again brought by the ſame gentlemen, and placed in the window.

At this juncture the Suba, who had received an account of the havock death had made amongſt us, ſent one of his Jemmautdaars to inquire if the Chief ſurvived. They ſhewed me to him; told him I had appearance of life remaining, and believed I might recover if the door was opened very ſoon. This anſwer being returned to the Suba, an order came immediately for our releaſe; it being then near ſix in the morning.

The freſh air at the window ſoon brought me to life; and a few minutes after the departure of the Jemmautdaar, I was reſtored to my ſight and ſenſes. But oh! Sir, what words ſhall I adopt to tell you the whole that my ſoul ſuffered at reviewing the dreadful deſtruction round me? I will not attempt it; and indeed, tears, (a tribute I believe I ſhall ever pay to the remembrance of this ſcene, and to the memory of thoſe brave and valuable men) ſtop my pen.

The little ſtrength remaining amongſt the moſt robuſt who ſurvived, made it a difficult taſk to remove the dead piled up againſt the door; ſo that I believe it was more than twenty minutes before we obtained a paſſage out for one at a time.

I had ſoon reaſon to be convinced the particular inquiry made after me, did not reſult from any dictate of favour, humanity, or contrition; when I came out, I found myſelf in a high putrid fever, and, not being able to ſtand, threw myſelf on the wet graſs without the Veranda, when a meſſage was brought me, ſignifying I muſt immediately attend the Suba. Not being capable of walking, they were obliged to ſupport me under each arm, and, on the way, one of the Jemmautdaars told me, as a friend, to make a full confeſſion where the treaſure was buried in the fort, or that in half an hour I ſhould be ſhot off from the mouth of a cannon *. The intimation gave me no manner of concern; for, at that juncture, I ſhould have eſteemed death the greateſt favour the tyrant could have beſtowed upon me.

Being brought into his preſence, he ſoon obſerved the wretched plight I was in, and ordered a large folio volume, which lay on a heap of plunder, to be brought for me to ſit on. I endeavoured two or three times to ſpeak, but my tongue was dry and without motion. He ordered me water. As ſoon as I got ſpeech, I began to recount the diſmal cataſtrophe of my miſerable companions. But he ſtopt me ſhort, with telling me, he was well informed of great treaſure being buried, or ſecreted, in the fort, and that I was privy to it; and if I expected favour, muſt diſcover it.

I urged every thing I could to convince him there was no truth in the information; or that if any ſuch thing had been done, it was without my knowledge. I reminded him of his repeated aſſurance to me, the day before; but he reſumed the ſubject of the treaſure, and all I could ſay ſeemed to gain no credit with him. I was ordered priſoner under Mhir Muddon, General of the Houſhold Troops.

Amongſt the guard which carried me from the Suba, one bore a large Moratter battle-ax, which gave riſe I imagine to Mr. Secretary Cooke's belief and report to the fleet, that he ſaw me carried out, with the edge of the ax towards me, to have my head ſtruck off. This I believe is the only account you will have of me, until I bring you a better myſelf. But to reſume my ſubject: I was ordered to the camp to Mhir Maddon's quarters, within the outward ditch, ſomething ſhort of Omychund's garden (which you know, is above three miles from the fort) and with me Meſſieurs Court, Walcot, and Burdet. The reſt, who ſurvived the fatal night, gained their liberty, except Mrs. Carey, who was too young and handſome. The dead bodies were promiſcuouſly thrown into the ditch of our unfiniſhed ravelin, and covered with the earth.

My being treated with this ſeverity, I have ſufficient reaſon to affirm, proceeded from the following cauſes. The Suba's reſentment for my defending the fort, after the governor, &c. had abandoned it; his prepoſſeſſion touching the treaſure; and thirdly, the inſtigations of

Omychund * in resentment for my not releasing him out of prison, as soon as I had the command of the fort: a circumstance, which in the heat and hurry of action, never once occurred to me, or I had certainly done it; because I thought his imprisonment unjust. But that the hard treatment I met with, may truly be attributed in a great measure to his suggestions and insinuations, I am well assured, from the whole of his subsequent conduct; and this further confirmed to me, in the three gentlemen selected to be my companions, against each of whom he had conceived particular resentment; and you know Omychund can never forgive.

We were conveyed in a Hackery † to the camp the 21st of June, in the morning, and soon loaded with fetters, and stowed all four in a seapoy's tent, about four feet long, three wide, and about three high; so that we were half *in*, half *out*: All night it rained severely.

* A great Gentoo merchant of Calcutta.

† A coach drawn by oxen.

ly. Diſmal as this was, it appeared a paradiſe compared with our lodging the preceding night. Here I became covered from head to foot with large painful boils, the firſt ſymptom of my recovery; for until theſe appeared, my fever did not leave me.

On the morning of the 22d, they marched us to town in our fetters, under the ſcorching beams of an intenſe hot ſun, and lodged us at the Dock-head in the open ſmall Veranda, fronting the river, where we had a ſtrong guard over us, commanded by Bundo Sing Hazary, an officer under Mhir Muddon. Here the other gentlemen broke out likewiſe in boils all over their bodies (a happy circumſtance, which as I afterwards learned, attended every one who came out of the Black-Hole).

On our arrival at this place, we ſoon were given to underſtand, we ſhould be embarked for Muxadabad *, where I think you have never been; and ſince I have brought you thus far, you may as well

* The capital of Bengal.

well take this trip with us likewiſe. I have much leiſure on my hands at preſent; and, you know, you may chuſe your leiſure for peruſal.

We ſet out on our travels from the Dock-head the 24th in the afternoon, and were embarked on a large Wollack*, containing part of Bundo Sing's plunder, &c. She bulged a-ſhore a little after we ſet off, and broke one of her floor timbers: however they puſhed on, tho' ſhe made ſo much water ſhe could hardly ſwim. Our bedſtead and bedding were a platform of looſe unequal bamboos laid on the bottom timbers: ſo that when they had been negligent in bailing, we frequently waked with half of us in the water. We had hardly any cloaths to our bodies, and nothing but a bit of mat, and a bit or two of old gunny-bag, which we begged at the Dock-head to defend us from the ſun, rains, and dews. Our food only rice, and the water along-ſide, which you know: is neither very clean, nor very palatable in the rains:

* A large boat.

rains: but there was enough of it without ſcrambling.

In ſhort, Sir, though our diſtreſſes in this ſituation, covered with tormenting boils, and loaded with irons, will be thought, and doubtleſs were, very deplorable; yet the grateful conſideration of our being ſo providentially a remnant of the ſaved, made every thing elſe appear light to us. Our rice and water-diet, deſigned as a grievance to us, was certainly our preſervation: for could we (circumſtanced as we were) have indulged in fleſh and wine, we had died beyond all doubt.

When we arrived at Hougly fort, I wrote a ſhort letter to Governor Biſdom (by means of a pencil and blank leaf of a volume of Archbiſhop Tillotſon's ſermons, given us by one of our guard, part of his plunder) adviſing him of our miſerable plight. He had the humanity to diſpatch three ſeveral boats after us, with freſh proviſions, liquors, cloaths, and money; neither of which reached us. But, "Whatever is, is right."

Our rice and water were more ſalutary and proper for us.

Matter ridiculous and droll abundantly occurred in the courſe of our trip. But theſe I will poſtpone for a perſonal recital, that I may laugh with you, and will only mention, that MY hands alone being free from impoſthumes, I was obliged for ſome time to turn nurſe, and feed my poor diſtreſſed companions.

When we came oppoſite to Santipore, they found the Wollack would not be able to proceed further, for want of water in the river; and one of the guard was ſent a-ſhore to demand of the Zemindar * of that diſtrict, light boats to carry priſoners of ſtate under their charge to Muxadabad. The Zemindar, giving no credit to the fellow, muſtered his guard of pykes, beat him, and drove him away.

This, on the return of the Burkandaſs, raiſed a moſt furious combuſtion. Our Jemmautdaar ordered his people to arms, and the reſolution was to take the Zemindar and carry him bound a pri-

G ſoner

* A proprietor of land.

ſoner to Muxadabad. Accordingly they landed with their fire-arms, ſwords, and targets; when it occurred to one miſchievous mortal amongſt them, that the taking me with them, would be a proof of their commiſſion, and the high offence the Zemindar had committed.

Being immediately lugged a-ſhore, I urged the impoſſibility of my walking, covered as my legs were with boils, and ſeveral of them in the way of my fetters; and intreated if I muſt go, that they would for the time take off my irons, as it was not in my power to eſcape from them; for they ſaw I was hardly able to ſtand. But I might as well have petitioned tygers, or made ſupplication to the wind. I was obliged to crawl: They ſignified to me, it was now my buſineſs to obey, and that I ſhould remember, I was not then in the Kella of Allynagore *. Thus was I marched in a ſcorching ſun, near noon, for more than a mile and half; my legs running in

* The name given to Calcutta, by the Suba, after the capture.

n a ſtream of blood from the irritation of my irons, and myſelf ready to drop every ſtep with exceſſive faintneſs and unſpeakable pain.

When we came near the Cutcherry of the diſtrict, the Zemindar with his pykes, was drawn up ready to receive us; but as ſoon as they preſented me to him as a priſoner of ſtate, eſtimated and valued to them at four lack of rupees*, he confeſſed himſelf ſenſible of his miſtake, and made no further ſhew of reſiſtance. The Jemmautdar ſeized him, and gave orders to have him bound and ſent to the boat: but on his making further ſubmiſſion, and promiſing to get boats from Santipore to ſend after us, and agreeing to pay them for the trouble he had cauſed, he was releaſed, and matters accommodated.

I was become ſo very low and weak by this cruel travel, that it was ſome time before they would venture to march me back; and the "ſtoney-hearted villains," for their own ſakes, were at laſt obliged to carry me part of the way, and

 ſupport

* 50,000 l.

ſupport me the reſt, covering me from the ſun with their ſhields. A poor fellow, one of our Under-Gomaſtaus of Santipore, ſeeing me at the Cutcherry, knew me, and, with tears in his eyes, preſented me with a bunch of plantains, the half of which my guard plundered by the way.

We departed from hence directly, in expectation of boats following us, but they never came; and the next day (I think the laſt of June) they preſſed a ſmall open fiſhing-dingy, and embarked us on that, with two of our guard only; for in fact, any more would have ſunk her. Here we had a bed of bamboos, ſomething ſofter, I think, than thoſe of the great boat; that is, they were ſomething evener, but were ſo diſtreſſed for room, that we could not ſtir without our fetters bruiſing our own, or each others boils; and were in woeful diſtreſs indeed, not arriving at Muxadabad until the 7th of July in the afternoon. We were all this while expoſed to one regular ſucceſſion of heavy rain, or intenſe ſun-ſhine, and nothing to defend us from either.

But then don't let me forget our bleſſings : for by the good-nature of one of our guard, Shaike Bodul, we now and then latterly got a few plantains, onions, parched rice, with Jaggree *, and the bitter green, called Curella : all which were to us luxurious indulgences, and made the rice go down deliciouſly.

On the 7th of July, early in the morning, we came in ſight of the French factory. I had a letter prepared for Mr. Law the Chief, and prevailed with my friend Bodul, to put to there. On the receipt of my letter, Mr. Law, with much politeneſs and humanity, came down to the water-ſide, and remained near an hour with us. He gave the Shaike a genteel preſent for his civilities, and offered him a conſiderable reward and ſecurity, if he would permit us to land for an hour's refreſhment : but he replied, his head would pay for the indulgence. After Mr. Law had given us

* Molaſſes.

us a ſupply of cloaths, linen, proviſions, liquors, and caſh, we left his factory with grateful hearts and compliments.

We could not, as you may imagine, long reſiſt touching on our ſtock of proviſions; but however temperate we thought ourſelves, we were all diſordered more or leſs by this firſt indulgence. A few hours after I was ſeized with a painful inflammation in my right leg and thigh.

Paſſing by our fort and factory at Coſſimbuzar, raiſed ſome melancholy reflections amongſt us. About four in the afternoon we landed at Muxadabad, and were conducted to, and depoſited in an open ſtable, not far from the Suba's palace in the city.

This march, I will freely confeſs to you, drew tears of diſdain and anguiſh of heart from me: thus to be led like a felon, a ſpectacle to the inhabitants of this populous city! My ſoul could not ſupport itſelf with any degree of patience; the pain too ariſing from my boils, and inflammation of my leg, added not a little, I believe, to the depreſſion of my ſpirits.

Here we had a guard of Moors placed on one ſide of us, and a guard of Gentoos on the other; and being deſtined to remain in this place of purgatory, until the Suba returned to the city, I can give you no idea of our ſufferings. The immenſe crowd of ſpectators, who came from all quarters of the city to ſatisfy their curioſity, ſo blocked us up from morning till night, that I may truly ſay we narrowly eſcaped a ſecond ſuffocation, the weather proving exceeding ſultry.

The firſt night after our arrival in the ſtable, I was attacked by a fever; and that night and the next day, the inflammation of my leg and thigh greatly increaſed: but all terminated the ſecond night in a regular fit of the gout in my right foot and ankle; the firſt and laſt fit of this kind I ever had. How my irons agreed with this new viſitor I leave you to judge; for I could not by any intreaty obtain liberty for ſo much as that poor leg. Dur-

During our reſidence here, we experienced every act of humanity and friendſhip from Monſ. Law and Mynheer Vernet, the French and Dutch Chiefs of Coſſimbuzar, who left no means uneſſayed to procure our releaſe. Our proviſions were regularly ſent us from the Dutch Tankſall * in Coriemabad; and we were daily viſited by Meſſrs. Roſs and Ekſtone, the Chief and Second there; and indeed received ſuch inſtances of commiſeration and affection from Mynheer Roſs, as will ever claim my moſt grateful remembrance.

The whole body of Armenian merchants too were moſt kind and friendly to us; particularly Aga Manuel Satoor: we were not a little indebted to the obliging good-natured behaviour of Meſſrs. Haſtings and Chambers, who gave us as much of their company as they could. They had obtained their liberty by the French and Dutch Chiefs becoming bail for their appearance. This ſecurity was often tendered for us, but without effect.

* The Dutch mint near Muxadabad.

The 11th of July the Suba arrived in the city, and with him Bundoo Sing, to whoſe houſe we were removed that afternoon in a Hackery; for I was not able to put my foot to the ground. Here we were confirmed in a report which had before reached us, that the Suba, on his return to Houghly, made inquiry for us when he releaſed Meſſieurs Watts and Collett, &c. with intention to releaſe us alſo; and, that he had expreſſed ſome reſentment at Mhir Muddon for having ſo haſtily ſent us up to Muxadabad. This proved a very pleaſing piece of intelligence to us; and gave us reaſon to hope the iſſue would be more favourable to us than we expected.

Though we were here lodged in an open Bungulo only, yet we found ourſelves relieved from the crowd of people which had ſtifled us at the ſtable, and once more breathed the freſh air. We were treated with much kindneſs and reſpect by Bundoo Sing, who generally paſſed ſome time or other of the day with us, and feaſted us with hopes of been ſoon releaſed.

The 15th we were conducted in a hackery to the Kella §, in order to have an audience of the Suba, and know our fate. We were kept above an hour in the ſun oppoſite the gate, whilſt here we ſaw ſeveral of his miniſters brought out diſgraced, in the cuſtody of Sootapurdars, and diſmiſſed from their employs, who but a few minutes before we had ſeen enter the Kella in the utmoſt pomp and magnificence.

Receiving advice, that we ſhould have no audience or admittance to the Suba that day, we were depoſited again at our former lodgings, the ſtable; to be at hand, and had the mortification of paſſing another night there.

The 16th in the morning an old female attendant on *Allyverdy Cawns Begum* ‡, paid a viſit to our Shaike, and

§ The ſeat of the Suba's reſidence in the city of Muxadabad.

‡ The dowager princeſs grandmother of Surajud Dowla.

diſcourſed half an hour with him. Overhearing part of the converſation to be favourable to us, I obtained the whole from him; and learned, that at a feaſt the preceding night, the *Begum* had ſollicited our liberty, and that the Suba had promiſed he would releaſe us on the morrow. This, you will believe, gave us no ſmall ſpirits; but at noon all our hopes were daſhed by a piece of intelligence from Bundoo Sing, implying, that an order was prepared, and ready to paſs the ſeal, for returning us in irons to Rajah Monickchund, governor of Allynâgore, the name the Suba had given to Calcutta.

I need not tell you what a thunderclap this proved to us in the very height of our flattering expectations; for I was, as to myſelf, well convinced I ſhould never have got alive out of the hands of that rapacious harpy, who is a genuine Hindoo †, in the very worſt acceptation of the word; therefore, from that moment gave up every hope of liberty.

† Hindoo or Gentoo.

Men in this ſtate of mind are generally pretty eaſy: it is hope which gives anxiety. We dined and laid ourſelves down to ſleep; and for my own part I never enjoyed a ſounder afternoon's nap.

Towards five the Shaike waked me with notice, that the Suba would preſently paſs by to his palace of Mooteejeel. We rouſed, and deſired the guard would keep the view clear for us. When the Suba came in ſight, we made him the uſual Salaam; and when he came abreaſt of us, he ordered his litter to ſtop, and us to be called to him. We advanced; and I addreſſed him in a ſhort ſpeech, ſetting forth our ſufferings, and petitioned for our liberty. The wretched ſpectacle we made, muſt, I think, have made an impreſſion on a breaſt the moſt brutal; and if he is capable of pity or contrition, his heart felt it then. I think it appeared in ſpight of him in his countenance. He gave me no reply: but ordered a Sootapurdar and Chubdaar, immediately to ſee our irons cut off, and to conduct us wherever we choſe to go, and to take care we received no trouble nor inſult; and having repeated this order diſtinctly, directed his retinue to go on. As ſoon as our legs were free we took boat, and proceeded to the Tank-fall, where we were received and entertained with real joy and humanity.

Thus, my worthy friend, you ſee us reſtored to liberty, at a time when we could entertain no probable hope of ever obtaining it. The foundation of the alarm at noon was this: Moneloll, the Suba's Dewan, and ſome others, had in the morning taken no ſmall pains to convince the Suba, "That, notwithſtand-"ing my loſſes at *Allynagore*, I was ſtill "poſſeſſed of enough to pay a conſide-"rable ſum for my freedom; and ad-"viſed the ſending me to *Monickchund*, "who would be better able to trace out "the remainder of my effects." To this I was afterwards informed the Suba replied. "It may be; if he has any "thing left, let him keep it: his ſuffer-"ings have been great; he ſhall have "his liberty." Whether this was the reſult of his own ſentiments, or the conſequence of his promiſe the night before to the old *Begum*, I cannot ſay; but, believe, we owe our freedom partly to both.

Being myſelf once again at liberty, it is time I ſhould releaſe you, Sir, alſo from the unpleaſing travel I have led you in this narrative of our diſtreſſes, from our entrance into that fatal Black-Hole. And, ſhall it after all be ſaid, or even thought, that I can poſſibly have arraigned or commented too ſeverely on a conduct which alone plunged us into theſe unequalled ſufferings? I hope not.

I am,

DEAR SIR,

Your moſt faithful and

obedient humble Servant,

J. Z. HOLWELL.

LIST of the SMOTHERED in the BLACK-HOLE Prison (exclusive of Sixty-nine, consisting of Dutch and English Serjeants, Corporals, Soldiers, Topaz's, Militia, Whites, and Portugueze) whose Names I am unacquainted with, making on the whole, One hundred and twenty-three Persons.

Of Counsel.

E. Eyre } Esqs;
Wm. Baillie }

The Rev. Jervas Bellamy.

Gentlemen in the Service.

Messrs. Jenks
Revely
Law
Coales, Ens. Mil.
Valicourt
Jebb
Toriano
E. Page
S. Page
Grub
Street.

Messrs. Harod
P. Johnstone
Ballard
N. Drake
Carse
Knapton
Gosling
Bing
Dod
Dalrymple.

Military Captains.

Clayton
Buchanan

Witherington

Lieutenants.

Bishop
Hays
Blagg

Simson
Bellamy.

Ensigns.

Paccard	C. Wedderburn
Scot	Dumbleton, Enſ. Mil.
Haſtings	

Serjeants, &c.

Serjeant Major	Abraham } Serjeants of Militia.
Quarter-Maſter Serjeant	Cartwright
	Bleau

Sea Captains.

Hunt	Guy
Osburne	Porter
Purnell, ſurvived the night, but died next day.	W. Parker
	Caulker
	Bendall
Meſſrs. Carey	Atkinſon
Stephenſon	Leech, &c. &c.

LIST of thoſe who SURVIVED the BLACK-HOLE Priſon.

Meſſrs. Holwell	Capt. Dickſon
Court	Mr. Moran
Secretary Cooke	John Meadows and 12 Military and Militia Blacks and Whites, ſome of whom recovered when the door was open.
Luſhington	
Burdet	
Enſ. Walcott	
Mrs. Carey	
Capt. Mills	

THE END.

James Bristow

A Narrative of the Sufferings of James Bristow belonging to the Bengal Artillery during Ten Years Captivity with Hyder Ali and Tippoo Saheb. London: John Murray, 1793.

CHAP. III.

Removal of the priſoners from Seringapatam to Myſore—various expeditions of Tippoo againſt the tributaries of the Nizam—cruel treatment of the priſoners—marriage of Tippoo's eldeſt ſon—his intolerance to his Hindoo ſubjects—his attack upon the Rajah of Travancore—rupture between him and the Engliſh—approach of General Meadows—action with Colonel Floyd—the priſoners conducted to the hill forts.

IN the month of December following, all the circumciſed Europeans in Seringapatam were removed to Myſore, the ancient capital of the kingdom, but at that time an inſignificant little fort about ſeven miles to the ſouthward of Seringapatam, which Tippoo has ſince demoliſhed, and erected a new and ſtronger one a little to the eaſtward of the former, called Sultan Killah. On our arrival here, we were cloſely confined, and in the very room where Captain Rumley and Lieutenants Frazer and Sampſon, whoſe deaths had already been whiſpered about the city, were murdered, ſhortly before, by the order of Tippoo.

When we diſcovered ourſelves to be not only in the ſame danger, but guarded by the very ſame aſſaſſins who had imbrued their hands in the blood of theſe gentlemen, we could no longer ſuppreſs our terrors. It now recurred to us what had often been aſſerted, that

Tippoo never would ſuffer any Britiſh captives to return, being determined to put all ſuch to death who ſhould ſurvive his cruel treatment. The murder of General Matthews's officers, which had been circulated at Seringapatam, and was credited by us all, contributed to confirm this ſuſpicion. In ſhort, it appeared evident that our extirpation was reſolved upon, on which account we unanimouſly determined to annihilate as many of Tippoo's hired aſſaſſins as we could, until ſuperior numbers ſhould cruſh us. At this time, however, our alarms proved groundleſs, and Tippoo's real view in ſending us hither, ſeemed to be nothing more than to keep us out of the way whilſt peace was in agitation, that we might have no opportunity of making our ſituations known, and conſequently be included in the number of thoſe who at laſt eſcaped his clutches. It is impoſſible, however, to determine what would have been our fate, had our releaſe been inſiſted on with ſufficient earneſtneſs to provoke his anger.

The commander of our guard had a ſlave, from whom we learnt the following particulars concerning the deteſtable murder of the above-mentioned gentlemen. Captain Rumley, when he found that he would be conſtrained to ſwallow poiſon, put an end to his own exiſtence rather than ſubmit; and Lieutenant Sampſon, having ſnatched up a large piece of wood that chanced to be within his reach, laid ſo furiouſly and reſolutely about him, that the cowardly murderers, afraid of approaching, threw a ſtone at him from ſome diſtance, which met his head with a mortal blow. Lieutenant Frazer alone was ſecured, and had poiſon forced down his throat, of which he ſoon after died.

After four months confinement at Myſore we were marched back to Seringapatam. Tippoo had then returned to his capital, and peace with the Engliſh was concluded. Our numbers at this time amounted to eighty, being the ſurvivors of ſuch as from time to time had been dragged out of the Seringapatam priſons, and circumciſed. The ſeamen, except thoſe ſelected for the palace, are included in this liſt. I have ſince learnt, that every priſon throughout the tyrant's dominions had in like manner been drained of the ill-fated Engliſhmen that were detained in captivity.

It is difficult for thoſe who never experienced ſimilar calamities to form any adequate or juſt conception of our deſpondence, in finding ourſelves, when peace was reſtored, for ever ſecluded from our country and friends. The hopes of one day rejoining thoſe to whom we might relate our adverſities in ſafety, and enjoy the pleaſing reflections of having ſurmounted ſufferings incurred in the cauſe and ſervice of our country, had hitherto ſupported us againſt every misfortune. A general reſtoration of priſoners had been the baſis of the peace, but our rulers found themſelves reduced to connive at the moſt flagrant infringement of this article.

We were now poſted to the different *Chaylah* battalions in the capacity of havildars, and received ſeven rupees per month. Lieutenants Speediman and Rutledge were appointed ſubadars. Lieutenant Brunton, who came up to Seringapatam at the ſame time with myſelf, and Enſign Gordon, a gentleman who had been a long time confined at Chittledroog, were liberated.

When I was moved to Myſore, two Europeans, one named O'Bryan, from the ſame company of Bengal artillery to which I had belonged, the other a ſerjeant of the Madras eſtabliſhment, taken in the Pollams, where Colonel Owen commanded, were compelled to perform the office of common coolies, and to carry dirt in the ſtreets of Seringapatam, becauſe they had attempted to eſcape ſhortly after they were captured, and at that time killed or wounded one or two of the guards that ſurprized them. On my return theſe two men exiſted no more; they had been aſſaſſinated by the ſultan's order, together with a native girl and two children belonging to the ſerjeant.]

Our confinement was ſtill continued with its former rigour and circumſpection; we were ſcarcely allowed, at firſt, to look out of our priſon, and for near three years ſucceeding the peace our ſlavery ſuffered little or no relaxation. We were not, in general, allowed to ſtir, even on the moſt preſſing occaſions, without a ſentry to accompany us; nor ſhould we at any time during that period have been permitted to walk about freely, if the officers who were entruſted with the charge of us, and reſponſible for our appearance, had not at times indulged us with with ſome liberty, truſting, I ſuppoſe, to the impoſſibility of our getting away.

Our firſt excurſion, after being repoſted in the manner already mentioned to the *Chaylah* battalions, was to a ſmall fort called Chindrapattah, on the Bedanore road, about twenty miles weſtward of Seringapatam, where we remained inactive during ſix months, and were then remanded to Seringapatam. During our ſtay at Chindrapattah, Enſign Clark, who held no higher ſtation than one of us, expired in conſequence of a violent beating from one of the ſubadars, whoſe cruelty he had provoked by ſome retorting language. Mr. Clark's body turned entirely black before he died, but no inquiry was inſtituted in conſequence, our lives not being of ſufficient importance to cauſe an inveſtigation. Mr. Ediman, the midſhipman, likewiſe quitted his miſerable exiſtence at this place, of a natural death indeed, but very prematurely brought on.

When we returned to Seringapatam, we were transferred from the *Chaylahs* to the Malabar Roman Catholic Chriſtians, conſiſting originally of about 40,000 unfortunate wretches, men, women, and children, forced away from the Bedanore and Mangalore countries in 1784, and compelled to embrace Mahometiſm, not, however, without exhibiting ſeveral martyrs in ſupport of a doctrine with which they had no farther acquaintance than what conſiſted in counting a row of beads, and performing genuflexions before a crucified image. The corps, or battalion of theſe wretches, to which I had been poſted, was ſoon afterwards ſent to Myſore, where it remained five months, and then returned. Theſe marches had nothing in view but to keep the unfortunate enſlaved ſoldiers (a name which they, however, did not deſerve) in employ, and to break any combinations which might have been formed.

The Engliſh peace concluded in 1784, no ſooner left Tippoo at liberty, than his turbulent ſpirit preſented as a convenient object for his rapacious ambition, the territories of Mouberjung, lying about twenty days journey to the northward of Seringapatam, and tributary to the nizam. Tippoo accordingly marched (the desire of conquest being a sufficient reason with him for making war) with an army, computed to be one hundred thousand strong, against Mouberjung's capital, called after the country Hydona, to which he laid siege after having subjected the frontiers, through which he spread terror and devastation. The nizam sent a body of cavalry to the assistance of Mouberjung, which induced Tippoo to abandon the siege; but he had already, it seems, impressed the latter with fears too lively to be erazed, The coast was therefore no sooner clear, before Mouberjung decamped to Hydrabad with his family and jewels, which had already so narrowly escaped falling into the hands of the invader, leaving him to take undisturbed possession of the fort of Hydona, which he totally demolifhed, the pettah having been plundered and nearly confumed by fire in an affault prior to the arrival of the auxiliary troops. I collected this information from the Europeans whom Tippoo had carried along with him, four of the Malabar Chriftian battalions having been employed on this occafion, to which thirty of the captive Europeans were attached.

As it was difficult, in an enemy's country, to guard men who had both courage and cunning fufficient to attempt a flight, five of the employed Europeans found means to elude all the circumfpection and vigilance of their obfervers, and fled to Mouberjung. One of General Matthews's fervants was amongft thefe deferters. The fultan determined immediately to fend the remainder back loaded with chains, and under a very ftrict confinement, and purfuant to his conftant practice of wreaking his vengeance on the whole of us, theſe men no ſooner arrived at Seringapatam than we ſhared their fate. Amongſt many other ſevere puniſhments which we underwent on this occaſion, without having been admitted to a chance of ſharing in the tranſgreſſion of thoſe for whom we ſuffered, was that of reducing our late allowance to barely one ſeer of very bad rice daily, great part of which we were obliged to diſpoſe of ſolely to procure fire-wood and ſalt for the reſt.

Under the alarming apprehenſions which this circumſtance created, and when we expected nothing leſs than to be either maſſacred on the ſpot, or diſtributed among thoſe hill forts from which no unfortunate exile was ever known to return, our terror received additional force from the eſcape of two of our companions, who found means to paſs the ſentries in the night, and eſcaped, notwithſtanding the vigilance of their guards. The greateſt difficulty, it muſt be obſerved, conſiſted in getting out of priſon, for the inhabitants of Seringapatam had for many years been ſo familiarized to the ſight of Europeans in the ſtreets, that little obſtruction was to be apprehended from the people, many of them being our well-wiſhers. Our confinement became after this infinitely more ſtrict, and almoſt inſupportably oppreſſive. The very guards dreaded the charge of us, being puniſhed ſeverely for every one that eſcaped, and were conſequently inſtigated by fear as much as inclination to treat us harſhly. In ten days, however, one of the fugitives being brought back to Seringapatam, our ſituations were made leſs irkſome. Both had been retaken near Tellicherry, but one had availed himſelf of the opportunity, when he was drinking water out of the river, to knock down the centinel that accompanied him, and then plunged into it and ſwam away. The unfortunate fellow that was brought back paid for the natural privilege of having made uſe of his legs with his noſe and ears, after which he was led round the fort on a jack-aſs with his face to the tail, and condemned to labour among the native ſmiths, who obliged him to blow the bellows for them. No account was ever received of the other. Two of thoſe Europeans whom Tippoo employed as armourers alſo attempted to eſcape at this time by ſwimming over the Coleroon; but it happened unfortunately that a guard was placed on the very ſpot where they gained the land, by which their deſign was diſcovered. One of theſe men had formerly been a midſhipman, and died at Seringapatam in Auguſt 1790.

In this dreadful ſtate of ſuſpenſe we remained during five months, when Tippoo returned from the invaſion of Hydona. He had poſſeſſed himſelf on that expedition, beſides plunder, of a country extending about fifty or ſixty coſs beyond Copaul, and almoſt as far as the Kiſtna, having, independent of the greateſt part of Hydona, taken Durbar and other places from the Mahrattas, all of which he held in ſubjection until the preſent war broke out. It was ſaid, that Tippoo alledged the Nizam's refuſal of his daughter, and Mouberjung of his ſiſter, for his ſon, as a pretext for the war. The propoſal had been rejected with contempt, the young Myſorean being of too mean an origin to aſpire at mixing his blood with that which flowed in veins of ſuch high deſcent.

Soon after the tyrant's return we were divided into three parties and difperfed; one was fent to Bedanore, another to Chittledroog, which lies to the northward of Seringapatam, not far from Copaul, and the third, to which I belonged, remained in the city. Thofe that went away were in irons; we that were referved were at firft pofted to a battalion of *Coorikies*, a people lying in the woods, whom Tippoo had enflaved; but in confequence of the frequent complaints and unfavourable reprefentations which our black officers made of our conduct, we were fubdivided anew into four parties, one of which remained with the *Coorikies*, another was pofted to a battalion of *Moplas*, and the other two incorporated with the Malabar Chriftians. It was thought, not without fome reafon, that the fewer of us were together the more tractable we fhould be. As we had often experienced the vanity of expecting any other redreſs for the ill uſage and injuries of our commanders, than what we could procure for ourſelves, ſo, whenever twelve or fifteen of us were together, and they grew too intolerable, we uſed to beat the whole battalion, guards and all, out of the ſquare, and make terms before we ceaſed hoſtilities. I have frequently known theſe effects of mere deſpair take place, and the officers, aſhamed of their own puſillanimity, would not make theſe little mutinies known, but they took care, in general, to be even with us, and charged us with ſome other offence, of which we had never perhaps thought.

Our allowance, which ſince the peace had been ſeven rupees per month, unleſs when in diſgrace, was at this time reduced to ſix rupees in forty-five days, which is the term of Tippoo's military month, according to which he pays his troops: this paltry ſtipend was, however, irregularly paid, and never at a ſhorter period than fifty days, frequently a longer period, which was a ſmall addition to the month, of the paymaſter's contrivance, as it reduced us to extreme diſtreſs at times, and the neceſſity of borrowing the money from him which was actually due to us: this ſcheme was ſo much to his liking, that he frequently kept us in long arrears on pretence of being without money, in order to oblige us to have recourſe to his aid, which he afforded in conſideration of a deduction of one-half in advancing what it was his duty to have paid long before. [I ſhall here mention a ſpecies of unkingly chicanery, by which Tippoo himſelf manages to cheat his troops out of great part of their pay. He keeps them three or four months in arrears, or until they begin to be very much diſ-treſſed for money ; and then allows his treaſurer, or ſome other perſon, with his money, to make them advances at a very exorbitant diſcount till the pay is iſſued, which generally takes place ſoon afterwards, and the profits of this political robbery accrues to himſelf. When we now reflect that they are bound always to receive one-fourth of their pay in grain, which generally conſiſts of what has been damaged as ſtores, and which the ſepoys are obliged to throw away, and that the treaſurer, or pay-jobber, probably expects or exacts ſomething for himſelf over and above what goes into the ſultan's coffers, we may naturally conclude, that the army is neither well paid, nor well ſatisfied, and that nothing but fear, want of unanimity and bold leaders, not to omit the unqueſtionable vigilance and abilities of the tyrant, prevents them from revolting. I am confident, from what I have ſeen, that he will ſome time or other feel the ill effects of their diſcontent.

In conſequence of what has been ſaid, we found ourſelves ſo much diſtreſſed at one time for the moſt indiſpenſable neceſſaries of life, that our party ventured on a ſtep, for the ſake of procuring temporary relief, which expoſed the whole to the imminent danger of a moſt ignominious death. It was ſuggeſted to ſome one of the ingenious and bold priſoners, at the time of the Moherrum, to ſteal out of priſon in the night, and when riot and intoxication had lulled the pious Muſſulmen to reſt, to rob the temples of the little ſilver hands which are offered during the feſtival by the munificent bigots, and then to re-enter the priſon in the ſame clandeſtine manner. We were all privy to this daring enterprize, and were all to ſhare equal in the benefit of its ſucceſs; great precaution was therefore taken to avoid diſcovery, and to aſſiſt the reſolute undertaker in effecting his purpoſe unobſerved. I confeſs that I was not leſs rejoiced than aſtoniſhed at his good fortune when I ſaw him return before day, not only undiſcovered, but furniſhed with a dozen of the ſilver relicks which he had ſafely purloined. We melted down the ſilver with all imaginable ſecrecy, and ſold it ſome time afterwards, which afforded a very ſeaſonable relief. We had, however, never afterwards, even when leſs vigilantly watched, an opportunity of repeating this theft, the ſucceſs of which I never ſufficiently could admire, as mere deſpair had inſpired the attempt.

In the year 1788, ſix of Tippoo's chiefs and a bramin were hanged at Seringapatam for being ſuſpected of carrying on a treacherous correſpondence with the Engliſh. A letter to Lieutenant Rutledge had been found on the bramin, and interpreted by Serjeant Dempſter, who has ſince informed me that it was ſimply a letter from the gentleman's mother, or ſome other relation, which the bramin, who came from the Carnatic, had engaged to deliver, but that it was accompanied by a ſhort note from one of Lieutenant Rutledge's friends, lamenting that he was no longer able, from want of opportunities, to write to him as formerly. This note produced all the miſchief, for it betrayed a prior correſpondence, which was ſufficient to rouſe diſtruſt and ſuſpicion in the jealous mind of Tippoo. Lieutenant Rutledge was, in conſequence of this diſcovery, loaded with fetters, and ſent to Nundidroog, a high and ſcarped rock, where he was confined on the very ſummit under a little *chopper* or ſhed, raiſed for the purpoſe, and only allowed about the ſpace of ten yards to move in, with three quarters of a ſeer of *raggy* and a few chillies to ſubſiſt on. In this dreadful ſituation he ſpun out a miſerable exiſtence nearly two years, when he was ſhot on the rock, for contriving to tranſmit a written requeſt to borrow four fanams of the priſoners at Seringapatam. This unfortunate gentleman has left a ſon behind him in Tippoo's dominions. I learnt the particulars of Lieutenant Rutledge's death from a farrier who had been confined on the ſame rock, but removed to Seringapatam in conſequence of the indiſpoſition of one of Tippoo's favourite Arabian horſes, and is the only perſon, I have been informed, that was ever known to return from any of theſe forts. He declared, that he had been hoiſted up to the top blind-folded, that there is but one narrow path down, which he perceived completely lined with ſentries, and that a fort guarded the aſcent ſome diſtance below the ſummit. No perſon, he added, except their guards, could, or were allowed to approach the priſoners. We were, as uſual, all of us involved in Lieutenant Rutledge's diſaſter on the diſcovery of the letter, and puniſhed with cloſe confinement and the loſs of our allowance for two months, during which time we lived on charity, and learnt to ſubſiſt ſeveral days without food.

An European, named White, having eſcaped from Bangalore the firſt year after the peace, for the ſecond time, ſeven other European priſoners, alſo confined at that place, were, on account of this circumſtance, put in irons and ſent to Sunderdroog, a fort to the north-eaſt of Seringapatam, and about twenty miles to the weſtward of Bangalore.

Theſe unfortunate men continued under a very ſevere arreſt on one ſeer of *raggy* and half a pice per day for themſelves and families, (women and children that were taken with them) until the year 1789, when, after ſuffering during four years all the rigour of ſlavery, fetters, and hunger, they were finally dragged into the woods and hanged. Their women were afterwards brought to Seringapatam, and related the deplorable cataſtrophe of their maſters—Nothing could be more ſhocking, more inhuman, and more baſe, than to preſerve a tormenting exiſtence to innocent men ſeveral years, for the ſole purpoſe of murdering them at laſt.

I was never able to diſcover when or in what manner the above-mentioned White got into Tippoo's ſervice, but he was there when the war began, and tho' a Briton, he ſtrained every nerve to injure and diſtreſs the Engliſh captives.

Through his treachery it was difcovered, that the captive officers had contrived to carry on fome contraband tranfactions, which fubjected them to examinations and reftraints' they never could account for, and might have endangered their exiftence, had any difcoveries been made, as the tyrant wanted very little pretext for murdering men who were obnoxious to him. He originally perfuaded Tippoo to retain fuch of the prifoners as were mechanics, and pointed out thofe whom he judged fit objects for this purpofe. Many, therefore, are indebted to him and his diabolical exertions for the perpetual lofs of liberty, and finally of their lives. Tippoo was latterly much prejudiced againft this man, and would certainly, in fome degree, have beftowed on him the fate he deferved, by hanging him, had he not faved himfelf by flight, for he had played his patron ſeveral provoking tricks, particularly pretending ſkill in caſting cannon; for when Tippoo had expended a great deal of money on a foundry and the neceſſary requiſites, he manifeſted his ignorance in ſpoiling all the metal: I am happy to find this miſcreant is now a priſoner at Madras. The vexations reſulting from White's ſtupidity were amply compenſated, however, ſhortly after, by the arrival of thirty artiſts from France, ſent out by the court of Verſailles with a view to inſtruct Tippoo's ſubjects in manufactures, and aiding this Aſiatic ally of France with mechanical knowledge, which as yet has made ſlow progreſs in his own dominions, as well as every other part of India. They were, no doubt, an earneſt of the ſtipulated ſupport and aſſiſtance in the projected war with us, of which he has ſince been ſo juſtly diſappointed. Two men of each profeſſion, or trade, were ſent out, and conſiſted chiefly of ſuch as were not to be found amongſt his own ſubjects, namely, founders, glaſs-blowers, watch-makers, armourers, broad-cloth weavers, &c. amongſt the reſt five ſugar bakers, a doctor, and a ſurgeon—I believe theſe people arrived with the ambaſſadors.

In the beginning of 1789, ſix men, whom we had not heard of before, were brought from Chittledroog to Seringapatam; this ſufficiently evinces, that many more Europeans than what are ſuſpected are concealed in Tippoo's dominions. Theſe men were, ſoon after their arrival, carried out of the fort in irons into a wood near the iſland, where they were hanged. They had belonged to the Bedanore garriſon which capitulated: what induced the barbarous conqueror to murder theſe men in cold blood I never was able to diſcover.

Soon after Tippoo again collected his forces, amounting, if report may be credited, to above 100,000; it is difficult, however, to afcertain the real number of an Indian army, which is always magnified very much beyond its reality; it would feem that a lack, or 100,000, when applied to an army, has a very unlimited meaning, and fignifies nothing more than a pretty large body; for having fo frequently known the term applied to lefs than half the number, and fcarcely ever heard of an Indian army of any note which was not exaggerated, I conclude it to be no more than a figure by which the relator means to convey his alarms: it muft, notwithftanding, be confeffed, that a great body of troops were collected, and that eight battalions of *Chaylahs* accompanied them. Tippoo marched down the Gauts as foon as the army was equipped, without divulging his intentions.

We heard nothing of this new expedition, or Tippoo's movements, for a conſiderable time; when, at laſt, orders were received at the capital to prepare for the nuptials of his ſon, a ſtout boy about ſeventeen years of age, who was now to eſpouſe the daughter of the Queen of Cannanore, ſince the Nizam had diſdainfully rejected him for a ſon-in-law; orders were alſo received at the ſame time to arrange matters preparatory to the father's inauguration, as "*Sultaun of the Eaſt*," the title which he in future intended to aſſume, and in which quality he meditated nothing leſs than the ſubjection of all India. He likewiſe iſſued a proclamation, prohibiting all marriages in the kingdom of Myſore until ſuch time as the wedding of his ſon ſhould take place, being determined to celebrate that day by the consummation of 25,000 marriages at his own charge. To be ignorant of every other feature in the character of this extraordinary man, and to be informed of this circumstance alone, would certainly inspire a high opinion of his munificence, liberality, and philanthropy, but the moment we are told that he tarnished all the glory which accompanied such a splendid act, by a piece of contemptible, fanatical, and tyrannical despotism, compelling 100,000 of his defenceless Hindoo subjects to embrace Mahometism on the same day, our admiration changes into merited detestation.

It is his constant and favourite practice to insult and persecute the Hindoos on the score of religion: he has demolished many of their temples and sanctified places of worship, particularly a much-revered pagoda near the bazar of Seringapatam, where he found, it is aſſerted, 150,000 coined pagodas, buried under the ſtone out of which the oval was hewn. He frequently orders calves to be brought before the doors of their temples, and ſheds the ſacred blood under the very noſe of the offended deity. Such as are acquainted with the enthuſiaſtic attachment of the Hindoos to their ancient religion and its rites, and their veneration for both, will gueſs at the extreme horror with which ſuch frightful ſacrileges muſt fill them, and will eaſily be perſuaded that Tippoo, as I have once obſerved, is deteſted by the majority of his ſubjects, and will only aſcribe their patience and ſubmiſſion to the known indolence and abject tameneſs of the Indians, who are awed by the vaſt armies he has hitherto contrived to maintain, and the known ſeverity with which he ever puniſhes the bare appearance of defection.

His orders for the ſolemnization of the marriage created a general buſtle and tumult throughout the city; every individual that could perform any thing curious or clever was employed, not only on their new ſultan's account, but all ſuch as propoſed diſplaying their adulation, and court their ſovereign by magnificent preſents on the occaſion, and ſuch alſo as hoped, by a diſguiſed bribe, to inſinuate themſelves into favour, and pave the road to future preferment. The palace of old Hyder was demoliſhed, and in the rear of it was begun a more extenſive and magnificent one of a triangular form, and fronting a famous pagoda in the center of the fort: in this the proud Myſorean propoſed to be inaugurated. Having been preſented by the court of France with four large and curious cryſtal pedeſtals, theſe were to ſupport his throne. This royal ſeat was to be ſuperbly decorated, and built by Europeans; but neither the palace nor the throne were finiſhed when I left Seringapatam. The preſent war ſeems to have retarded theſe deſigns, and the intelligence of Tippoo's repulſe at the Travancore lines put a total ſtop to the immenſe preparations which for a time had engroſſed the whole attention of the capital; the wall that ſurrounded the area of the new palace was alone ſuffered to be finiſhed; it is one mile in circumference, with a large gate on each ſide, the principal and grandeſt of which faces the above-mentioned pagoda. It is very uncertain when the ſplendid edifice itſelf will be finiſhed, as all farther thoughts about it are ſuſpended, and will not be reſumed until the preſent war is terminated, on the iſſue of which Tippoo's future glory and fate ſeem to hang. So ſenſible and convinced was he of the deciſive conſequences of a war raſhly undertaken with reſpect to himſelf and his ambitious projects, that he no ſooner diſcovered the expected and ſtipulated aids from France would fail, and the exertions of his enemies ſo much exceed what he had believed, than he ſeriouſly repented his wanton breach of treaty, not from principles of good faith or juſtice, but from apprehenſion of its effects to his own intereſt: it is to be hoped, that he will never again remain in a ſtate to diſturb the tranquility of India.

The loſs of his great ſeal, turban, and palanquin, captured in the before-mentioned repulſe, together with ſeveral valuable jewels, and the narrow eſcape of his own perſon, had a very diſheartening tendency upon his creatures in the capital, and gave riſe to very ignominious interpretations from the diſcontented. It was allowed that he would certainly have fallen into his enemies hands if a mean diſguiſe had not protected him; the very bearers of his palanquin were cut down ſome moments after he had deſerted it; he was attempting to ſurprize a defended ditch at ſome diſtance from the Travancore lines, when this unexpected ſally was made, and had nearly put a period to his career.

Tippoo having thought proper to ſubſtitute another inſcription on his new ſignet, this circumſtance gave freſh alarms at Seringapatam, and many took it for granted the tyrant had been either killed or dethroned, and the ſupreme authority aſſumed by ſome other perſon; but the general anxiety diſſipated when a new ſtate palanquin was diſpatched with great pomp, to be the ſumptuous and future vehicle of an upſtart ſultan.

When he had carried the long-disputed point against Travancore, which took up about twice the time he had conjectured, he returned to his capital, and was received with all the splendour of a conqueror; triumphal arches filled the streets through which he passed, and the decorations which had been originally destined to grace the nuptials of his son, were displayed on this occasion. On his arrival he proceeded directly to his father's tomb, where he spent the whole day in solemn prayers. He entered the fort at night through a road brilliantly illuminated.

On his return from this expedition, he brought a number of different sorts of guns, and a large quantity of sheet copper, of which he had stripped the domes of the Roman Catholic churches on the Malabar coast; with likewise 3000 of the captured Travancorians and the families of about 300 of the

Cochin people, whom he had been cruel enough to ſeize, and after tying them in pairs, drove them into the ſea.

Tippoo now thought very ſeriouſly about new-modelling and muſtering his troops: that he placed no remarkable confidence in their loyalty and faith was evident from the precautions he took to prevent mutiny and revolt. He artfully put ſuch men together as were moſt likely never to join in any general diſaffection from mutual averſion and diſtruſt of each other; by which means all his corps were compoſed of different caſts, nations, and religions, that bore a natural antipathy, and ſometimes an avowed enmity, to each other: this might indeed, in ſome meaſure, remedy one evil, but ſowed the ſeeds of another, that of diſunion in their efforts, when it might be highly neceſſary that their joint exertions ſhould combine in the accomplishment of the same object. He augmented his *Chaylah* battalions from eight to thirty, observing the same mode with respect to embodying them, as with the regulars, which indeed may appear more reasonable to such as have no knowledge of the disposition of his standing army, a circumstance which Tippoo is perfectly well acquainted with.

The artillery did not escape his notice; his arsenal was well supplied with warlike stores, and every preparation in his power was made for a war; the English prisoners were ordered into the fort again, and their capturer, at one of the reviews, observing amongst the *Chaylahs* some prisoners that were shaved, he remarked to one of his courtiers: " These men, I see, have " discovered a new Bible and creed at " last," meaning the Koran and Mahomedan doctrine. When he had inſpected every thing in perſon, carried reform into every department, and provided againſt deficiencies and abuſes, he at laſt iſſued orders for a ſecond campaign, and took the field.

It was originally ſaid that he meant to go to the northward, and lead his army againſt the troops of Mouberjung and Captain Read's detachment, which had not been then joined by Perſuram Bhow, but the intelligence of General Meadows's approach to the Gauts, and the capture of Coimbatore, an event totally unexpected, produced a change in his determination. He immediately croſſed the Cavery, and fixed his camp to the ſouthward of Seringapatam. It was not, however, until they received the intelligence from an European taken priſoner at Caroor, where he had been ſtraggling whilſt intoxicated, and brought to Seringapatam, that the European priſoners heard for certain of war having actually broke out betwixt Tippoo and the English.

Before he took the field a second time, he ordered three Europeans, and a number of native prisoners, who had been in his father's and his own possession a considerable time, among whom were several native officers, a Nayar rajah, and a commandant on the Bombay establishment taken in Bedanore, to be sent to Nundydroog and other hill forts, where I conjecture they have since been murdered, as that is the usual fate of all those who are doomed to these places. The farrier already mentioned, whose life had been spared in compliment to one of Tippoo's horses, was of the number. He also sent back from his camp an European corps in which he placed no confidence, being commanded by one *Maclean*, who had been a serjeant in his Majeſty's ſervice, but deſerted from the garriſon of Mangalore when it was under the command of Major Campbell.

This corps conſiſted of nothing but vagabonds and deſerters, chiefly Portugueſe, French, Dutch, and Danes. It had been diſarmed and diſgraced during Tippoo's firſt abſence, being ſuſpected, and very juſtly, I believe, of having encouraged and promiſed aid to the different *Chaylah* corps, who intended to rebel during the abſence of the army, and emancipate themſelves; the accompliſhment of which plan nothing could have prevented, had they not deliberated till it got vent, and were deprived of their arms and ſecured, as well as all who were ſuſpected of abetting and forwarding their project. Tippoo, it is true, had re-armed Maclean's corps, but ſo humble was his opinion of their loyalty and bravery, that he judged it very unadviſeable to oppoſe them to the troops of an European power, ſo that they ſtill remained inactive at Seringapatam when I left it.

Tippoo is naturally of a ſuſpicious temper, which the knowledge of his being unpopular increaſes. The Europeans are peculiarly, and without exception, the objects as well of his deteſtation as diſtruſt, ſo much ſo, that I may ſafely aſſert, there is not at this moment a ſingle regiment in his ſervice commanded by an European officer, nor did he ever ſuffer Lally's army to multiply ſufficiently to be able to give him uneaſineſs. I do not think that Lally, at any one time ſince Hyder's death, has had more than between one and two thouſand men under his command, and thoſe were diſciplined and paid by himſelf; he has had latterly very few Europeans, not more than 150 on a large computation.

It was in the beginning of September 1790 that Tippoo directed his ſteps towards the Gauts; but no ſooner had he publiſhed his intention of facing General Meadows, before an univerſal diſcontent and fear, which manifeſted itſelf in loud murmurs, pervaded all ranks at Seringapatam, and it was reported that the army was not better ſatisfied. Thoſe who remained in the city were far from repoſing that confidence in his army which the tyrant flattered himſelf they would, and could not diveſt themſelves of the apprehenſion of an Engliſh ſiege, with the conſequences of falling into the hands of an enemy that had ſuch ample and juſt cauſe for vengeance. The army again dreaded an attack in deſcending the Gauts, which they already concluded were in General Meadows's poſſeſſion, and conſequently judged it impoſſible to eſcape a total defeat.

Tippoo received the firſt intelligence of Colonel Floyd's ſituation and ſtrength by two European deſerters from the grand army, and haſtened to intercept him, in the full perſuaſion of commencing this war with a ſecond Conjeveram buſineſs. That this depended much upon the criſis of that day cannot be denied, and that the bravery and exertions of the troops who reſiſted ſuch ſuperior force is as meritorious as it was important, will never be diſputed. The loſs which Tippoo ſuſtained in this attempt was induſtriouſly concealed, but it certainly was conſiderable, it being whiſpered at Seringapatam to exceed greatly in number the whole force that oppoſed it, notwithſtanding the exaggerated and diſcredited accounts which Tippoo tranſmitted of his boaſted victory. The earlieſt intelligence of the engagement was accompanied by the remains of five of Tippoo's principal officers, who had fallen in the action.

Nothing, I am well convinced, prevents many of his diſſatisfied ſubjects from deſerting at this preſent time, but the certain death or vaſſalage to which they would expoſe their wives and families, whom Tippoo always ſecures before he raiſes a perſon to any place or office of truſt, as hoſtages for his fidelity and good conduct.

Even the very favourable repreſentation of the rencounter with Colonel Floyd could not entirely baniſh the terror of a blockade from the Myſorean capital. Tippoo's obſtinate diſpoſition was no ſecret to his ſubjects, and the horrors of a ſiege, together with the exceſſes a large army confined to the limits of the iſland would commit, presented themselves in lively colours to the citizens, some of whom had beheld the scene once before, not to revive their alarms, and threaten them with the prospect of perishing, if no otherwise, by famine.

The late progress of the army beyond the Gauts, &c. has, no doubt, in part realised the fears of the Mysoreans, whose situation must be distressing; and I should not in the least be astonished, if the accumulation of their burdens and wants became (which cannot be very remote) so intolerably oppressive, that they positively refuse to submit to the tyrant, and surrender the capital. I am induced to form this conjecture from what I remarked when our forces were at a great distance, and when so many obstacles and impediments might still be thrown in their way. Tippoo then frequently found it necessary to put such persons clandestinely to death as ſhewed their diſſatisfaction and diſtruſt too openly, that they might not ſpread the contagion.

Tippoo had engaged Colonel Floyd with nearly the whole of his numerous and newly-recruited army; he had employed all his art and addreſs to magnify the advantages of a very fruitleſs and inglorious attempt; but when he diſcovered that the real ſtate of the affair was not to be diſguiſed, though few were hardy enough boldly to avow the truth, he ungenerouſly reſolved to avenge himſelf on the unfortunate priſoners for his miſcarriage, and hoped, by ſacrificing them, to appeaſe in ſome meaſure the friends of the ſlaughtered ſirdars. Purſuant to this reſolution, he ordered all the captives that were with the *Chaylahs*, beſides ſix of the moſt refractory tradeſmen, to be put in irons and conducted to the hills, preparatory, as was intimated to us by our guards, to our being offered up as victims to the manes of the deceafed.

Two days before this removal took place, I had hid myfelf in one of the cavaliers of the fort, terrified at the idea of vifiting the hill forts; but being much pinched by hunger, and reflecting that my abfence might accelerate whatever mifchief was deftined for thofe companions with whom I had been a fellow-fufferer for fo many years, I could not perfuade myfelf to abandon or expofe them to additional danger merely on my own account, I therefore delivered myfelf up on the day we marched, determined to meet whatever fate awaited me. Nothing but the remorfe which I felt at entailing on the other captives the certain refentment of a barbarian, whofe implacable difpofition was well known, prevented me and many others, I believe, from trying with more eagernefs than we had done to eſcape, hoping conſtantly that ſome fortunate moment, or unforeſeen change, would one day or other effect the releaſe of the whole of us at once; nor was it eaſy to reſiſt the earneſt prayers, entreaties, deſpondence, and ſometimes even threats of our wretched brethren in affliction, from whom it was difficult, and almoſt impracticable, to conceal any ſuch deſign; to this, in a great meaſure, may be attributed the very few deſertions that took place. Tippoo, without doubt, knew too well that nothing was more likely to ſecure his priſoners, than the anxiety they took for the ſafety of each other, a bond more binding than any fetters he could fix upon them. In the year 1787, five men beſides myſelf had actually reſolved to truſt our lives in a boat on the Coleroon, and let the current carry us where it would, though we had been informed that a cataract on the route rendered this enterprize extremely hazardous; but we were certain it would carry us from Seringapatam, and nothing which could befal us afterwards appeared half ſo dreadful as remaining in ſlavery there. We had nearly conſtructed a baſket-boat for our purpoſe, made of bamboos, which we got ready ſplit from the *Dhomwallas*, or baſket-makers, and had ſecured leather to cover it with. An old uninhabited houſe ſerved to hide our materials and machine in; the ſplit bamboos were concealed under the thatched roof, ſo as not to be immediately diſcovered by any perſon looking accidentally into the houſe. The boat itſelf was buried in a large hole in the ground. Two of us uſed to ſteal away for an hour or two in the night, and work by turns whenever we found it practicable. Is came, however, to the knowledge of the reſt, and alarmed them ſo much, that we yielded to their ſupplications, and abandoned the project, as it was impoſſible to build, or even procure, boats to convey the whole of us at one trip.

'Koregaon Battle'

Gazetteer of the Bombay Presidency 18, part 3.
Bombay: Government Central Press, 1885.

considerable obstruction to the progress of the detachment; and one attempt to communicate with the road leading to it from Poona proved ineffectual. Another avenue being found, Lieutenant-Colonel Prother came before the place on 11th March with an advance party which drove in the enemy's outposts,[1] leaving the remainder of the detachment to follow under Major Hall of His Majesty's 89th Foot which arrived on the following day with the exception of the heavy train. Even this had been greatly lightened by leaving at Lohogad two eighteen-pounders and one of the thirteen-inch mortars. On the 13th a fire from the smaller mortar opened against the place and produced immediately an evident conflagration, while another battery was in a state of forwardness, opposite the north-eastern gateway, which was the chief access to the fort. On the morning of the 14th at daybreak, this likewise opened with good effect from one thirteen, one ten, and two eight-inch mortars, and about seven in the evening the enemy's magazine was seen to blow up which laid the chief gateway in ruins and burnt several of their houses. This induced the garrison to demand a suspension of hostilities, which was followed an hour afterwards by their surrender. About 700 men supposed to include some of those who had fled from Visápur and Lohogad and the commandant Jánoba Bháu were taken prisoners. The loss of the detachment on this occasion was twelve men including one officer of Engineers slightly wounded, and that of the enemy about thirty-five most of whom were killed at the explosion. Treasure valued at about £10,000 (Rs. 1 *lákh*) and some grain were found in the fort. The fall of Koari was followed on the 17th by the surrender and occupation of the dependent fortress of Gangad about eight miles to the south.[2]

Koregaon village, twenty-five miles south-west of Sirur and about sixteen miles north-east of Poona, with in 1881 a population of 960, is famous for its successful defence on the 1st of January 1818 by 800 British troops against 30,000 Maráthás. Towards the end of December, in the pursuit of Bájiráv Peshwa which followed the battle of Kirkee (5th November 1817), news reached Colonel Burr, who was in charge of Poona, that Bájiráv was passing south from Junnar and meant to attack Poona. Colonel Burr sent to Sirur for help. The second battalion of the first regiment Bombay Native Infantry of 500 rank and file under Captain Francis Staunton, accompanied by 300 irregular horse and two six-pounder guns manned by twenty-four European Madras artillerymen under a serjeant and a Lieutenant, left Sirur for Poona at eight in the evening of the 31st of December. After marching all night, a distance of twenty-five miles, about ten in the morning, from the high ground

---

[1] For the reconnaissance and investment of the fort Lieutenant Remon of the Engineers and a party under Captain Rose of His Majesty's 89th Regiment were detached from Seruli six miles south-east of Koari on the morning of the 11th and they completely succeeded in their object of gallantly driving in the enemy who were advantageously posted on a height protected by a well directed fire from the fort guns. The besieging force with knapsacks on the shoulders of the men and after a march of six miles advanced to the charge up a steep hill to the very walls of the fort, the besieged keeping up a brisk fire of cannon and musketry. Bombay Courier, 28th March 1818.

[2] Blacker's Maráthá War, 247-248.

behind Talegaon Dhamdhere, they saw across the Bhima the Peshwa's army of 25,000 Marátha horse. Captain Staunton marched on as if to ford the river, then turned, and took the village. Koregaon was surrounded by a mud wall of no great strength.[1] Captain Staunton secured a strong position for his guns and awaited the enemy's attack. As soon as the Marátha horse saw the British they recalled a body of 5000 infantry which was some distance ahead. When the infantry arrived three parties, each of 600 choice Arabs Gosávis and regular infantry, under cover of the river bank and supported by two guns, advanced to storm the village on three points. A continued shower of rockets set on fire many of the houses. The village was surrounded by horse and foot and the storming party broke down the wall in several places and forced their way in and secured a strong square enclosure from which they could not be dislodged. Though the village stood on the river bank the besiegers cut them off from water. Wearied with their night's march, under a burning sun, without food and without water, a handful of men held an open village against an army. Every foot was disputed, several streets and houses were taken and retaken, but more than half the European officers being wounded, the Arabs made themselves masters of a small temple, where three of the officers were lying wounded. Assistant Surgeon Wingate, one of their number, got up, and went out, but was immediately stabbed by Arabs and his body mangled. Lieutenant Swanston, who had two severe wounds, advised his remaining companion to suffer the Arabs to rifle them, which they did but without further violence. In the meantime, a party of the battalion under Lieutenant Jones and Assistant Surgeon Wyllie, came to the rescue, retook the temple and carried their companions to a place of greater safety. Thirst drove the besieged nearly frantic and some of the gunners, all of whom fought with glorious bravery, thinking resistance hopeless, begged for a surrender. Captain Staunton would not hear of yielding. The gunners were still dissatisfied when their officer, Lieutenant Chisholm, happened to be killed and the enemy encouraged by his death rushed on one of the guns and took it. Lieut. Pattinson, Adjutant of the Second Battalion, a man six feet seven inches in height, of giant strength and heroic courage, was lying mortally wounded shot through the body. Hearing that the gun was taken he called on the Grenadiers once more to follow him, and seizing a musket by the muzzle, rushed into the thick of the Arabs and felled them right and left till a second ball through the body disabled him. He was nobly seconded, the gun was retaken, and dragged out of a heap of dead Arabs. Lieutenant Chisholm's body was found with the head cut off. This is the fate, cried Captain Staunton, of all who fall dead or alive into Marátha hands. The gunners took the lesson to heart and fought on with unflinching courage, and the defence did not slacken though only three officers, Captain Staunton, Lieutenant Jones, and Assistant Surgeon Wyllie, remained fit for duty. Towards evening their case seemed hopeless. As night fell the attack lightened and they

1 Grant Duff (Maráthás, 656) describes the wall as full of large breaches on the river side and completely open on the east. This was its state at the end of the siege.

got water. By nine the firing ceased and the Maráthás left. Of the 834 defenders of Koregaon 275 were killed, wounded and missing, of whom were twenty of the twenty-six gunners. The Maráthás lost between 500 and 600 killed and wounded.[1] In reward for the defence of Koregaon which General Sir T described as 'one of the most heroic and brilliant achievements ever recorded on the annals of the Army' the second battalion of the First Regiment was made Grenadiers as the first battalion had been made for the defence of Mangalur. The motto of the regiment became Mangalur and Koregaon.[2] Captain Staunton was appointed an honorary aide-de-camp to the Governor General and presented by the Court of Directors with a sword ornamented with a suitable inscription and a sum of 500 guineas. On attaining the rank of Major in 1823 Captain Staunton was appointed a companion of the Most Honourable the Military Order of the Bath.[3]

Mr. Elphinstone, who visited Koregaon two days after the fight (3rd January 1818), found every sign of violence and havoc. The houses were burnt and scattered with accoutrements and broken arms, and the streets were filled with the bodies of dead men and horses. The men were mostly Arabs and must have attacked most resolutely to have fallen in such numbers. Some wounded were treated with the same care as the British wounded. About fifty bodies within the village and half a dozen without, with the wounded and the dead, made not less than 300. About fifty bodies of sepoys and eleven Europeans, besides the officers, were found imperfectly buried.[4]

At[5] the eminence near the river is a round stone tomb, where the artillerymen killed in the action were buried. At this point the river is crossed, and 300 yards to the left of the Poona road on the opposite bank is an obelisk 65 feet high of which 25 feet is pediment 12' 8" square. It stands on a stone platform 32' 4" square. The obelisk is of polished hard stone, and is enclosed with a stone wall six feet high on three sides, and an iron railing with a handsome iron gate and two lamps on the west side. The inscription on the north and south sides is in Maráthi; and the inscription on the west side given below is in English. The inscription on the north and east sides gives the names of the English killed and wounded, and of four natives attached to the artillery who were killed, from which it appears that of the eight officers engaged three were killed and two wounded, and of the twenty English artillerymen eleven were killed. The English inscription on the west side is:

[1] The details are: Second battalion First Regiment, 500 rank and file and five officers, Captain Staunton, Lieutenant Pattinson killed, Lieutenant Conellan wounded, Lieutenant Jones, Assistant Surgeon Wingate, killed. Artillery, twenty-four men and two officers, Lieutenant Chisholm killed and Assistant Surgeon Wyllie. Auxiliary Horse 300 men and one officer, Lieutenant Swanston wounded. Grant Duff's Maráthás, 658 footnote 2.

[2] Grant Duff's Maráthás, 658 footnote 1.

[3] The sword was presented to Captain Staunton on the 1st of January 1820 by the Honourable Mountstuart Elphinstone. Five years later Lieutenant-Colonel Staunton, C.B., died on the 25th of June 1825 off the Cape of Good Hope. Historical Record, 2nd Grenadier Regiment, 19-34, 39.

[4] Colebrooke's Elphinstone, II. 16-17.

[5] Murray's Bombay Handbook, 304-305. Compare Jacquemont, Voyage dans l' Inde, III. 544.

This Column
is erected to commemorate the defence of Coregaum
by a Detachment commanded by Captain
Staunton of the Bombay Establishment
which was surrounded on the 1st of January 1818
by the Peshwa's whole army under his
personal command,
and withstood throughout the day a series of
the most obstinate
and sanguinary assaults of his best troops.
Captain Staunton,
under the most appalling circumstances,
persevered in his desperate resistance,
and, seconded by the unconquerable spirit of
his Detachment,
at length achieved the signal discomfiture of
the Enemy
and accomplished one of the proudest
triumphs
of the British Army in the East.

To perpetuate
the Memory of the brave troops
to whose heroic firmness and devotion it owes
the glory of that day,
the British Government
has directed the names of their Corps and of
the killed and wounded
to be inscribed on this monument.
MDCCCXXII.[1]

Kurkumb, a small village of 911 people, on the Poona-Sholápur road, seven miles south-east of Pátas station and about twenty miles north of Bárámati, has two temples built in honour of Phirangádevi, one in the village and the other on a neighbouring hill. The larger temple of cut and polished stone is eight-sided with an audience hall or *sabhámandap* and verandas on both sides. The other temple on the hill is smaller and was built by Sambháji Náik Nimbálkar, Deshmukh of Phaltan in 1759 (*Shak* 1681). It contains a Maráthi inscription in Devnágari characters dated *Shak* 1681 (A.D. 1759) recording the name and the pedigree of the builder of the temple.

About four miles south of the Kárle cave hills and eight miles south-east of Khandála, in the range that forms the southern limit of the Indráyani valley, stand two fortified hills, Lohogad to the west short and comb-backed, and Visápur long and level to the east. From the village of Bhája, about a mile south of the Kárle railway station, a path leads up the face of a slightly wooded spur to the plateau from which rise the sheer cliffs of Lohogad on the right, and the tamer sides of Visápur on the left. From the top of the pass, between two hills, the track divides, one branch running west below the cliffs of Lohogad, the other east below the slopes of Visápur. This is the simplest path up either of the hills and is open all through the fair season. During the hot months (March-May) the pleasantest way of seeing Lohogad and Visápur from Khandála or Lonávla, is to start from the western village of Avadholi, climb Lohogad from the south, and passing to Visápur, scramble up the steep rugged gorge in its south face, and, crossing the hill, return by the north ravine along a smooth

[1] Compare Chesson and Woodhall's Bombay Miscellany, VII. 46-48.

Julia Inglis

The Siege of Lucknow: A Diary.

London: James R. Osgood, McIlvine, 1895.

accepted in order to be near our husbands. We were very busy packing all the afternoon. Whilst we were at dinner, Major Banks came to speak to John; he was in a state of great excitement, said he considered the move to cantonments most injudicious, that the city Residency was the place in which we ought to have collected our forces, and to that we should hold on like grim death; he evidently considered we were in a critical and dangerous position.

The 32nd was ordered to march the next morning, the 17th (Sunday). Just as we were getting up, a note arrived for John from Captain Hayes to say we were likely to be attacked on entering cantonments. This was not pleasant news; however, I got myself and my three children ready as soon as possible, and John went off to the parade-ground. When ready I mounted my pony, and with Mrs. Case and her sister rode up and down the road near our bungalows, waiting for the order to march. Some of the police-force came up at this time to guard our houses. Day was just breaking; hardly a sound broke the stillness of the hour, for no bugles or drums were allowed to sound, in order that our time of march might not be known; and a sort of awe crept over us, giving us presentiments of evils to come. We waited nearly an hour, there having been some unaccountable delay in the march of the regiment. At last Colonel Case came for us. One troop of irregular cavalry, four guns, and the 32nd, composed our force. Mrs. Case, Miss Dickson, and I rode in front; Mrs. Giddings and my three boys were close to us in carriages; Colonel Case rode on to reconnoitre. The city was perfectly quiet as we passed through—indeed, all the inhabitants seemed asleep, and half-way from cantonments we met Sir Henry, who told us all was right, the report of an attack having been spread by a drunken artilleryman; so our alarm subsided. On reaching cantonments the regiment marched into camp, and we took up our quarters in Sir Henry's house. I think it was the longest day I ever passed, as of course we could settle to nothing. John came in the evening, and read the service with me; he told me he did not think we should ever return to our house. This was sad news, as we had imagined the fall of Delhi, against which a large force had been sent, would put an end to all fear of disturbances here. Mrs. Gall and Mrs. Barber, whose husbands were in the irregular cavalry, arrived here this evening, the place they lived in not being considered safe. Colonel Case dined with us. John remained in camp; being in command, he did not like to leave his regiment at night. I sat next Sir Henry; he was very grave and silent. He told me that he considered the annexation of Oude the most unrighteous act that was ever committed. A telegraphic message came in whilst we were at dinner, which we feared did not contain good news.

The next morning (19th), at eleven o'clock, an alarm was given that the 71st N.I. intended rising at two o'clock. The gentlemen immediately rushed out, and ladies from all parts rushed in for protection. We were all ordered, in case the house were attacked, to go into a small inner room without windows, and to remain there whilst the firing lasted. The hour passed, however, and all remained quiet. John had the regiment ready to turn out, and was standing by the guns when the hour struck, expecting the attack to be made; but the Sepoys remained passive. This alarm augmented the numbers in our house very much, and we were now eleven ladies and fifteen children. Sir Henry, notwithstanding all he had to do, spared no pains in making us as comfortable as circumstances would admit. I had a small room to myself with the children—a great comfort; but I did not quite like having a Sepoy of the 4th Oude Infantry as a sentry outside my door, which had no fastening. These Sepoys were most mild-looking men, and used to amuse themselves during the day by playing with the children. I used to watch them, and could hardly fancy they were murderously inclined.

The next day (20th) nothing eventful occurred. I paid Mrs. Hayes a visit, and found her sadly cast down and anxious. Sir Henry gave a large dinner-party. I think he was anxious to keep up our spirits, but the attempt was, I am sure, trying to him and to all of us. He received this day from Lord Canning the appointment of brigadier-general, which invested him with full powers, civil and military, and freed him from all control; this seemed to give him pleasure.

21st.—From the reports of spies an attack was expected to-day, but everything remained quiet till the evening, when, just as we were sitting down to dinner, Sir Henry and his staff were heard calling for their horses, and we caught the words, 'A fire in the artillery lines!' The table was at once abandoned, and everyone rushed to the door. Certainly the sight was alarming; the flames were rapidly spreading, and appeared to be coming in the direction of our house. It was considered as the signal for the outbreak of the mutiny, and fear was painted on every countenance. Some counselled our leaving the bungalow, and taking refuge elsewhere; but at that moment Mr. Polehampton, the chaplain, came in, and said we were all to remain where we were. The wind providentially died away, and the fire was got under. I shall never forget poor Sir Henry's look of relief when he returned and said all was right. It was almost the first time I had seen a smile on his countenance. John had the 32nd under arms, expecting to be attacked, but the Sepoys actually helped to put the fire out. At this time our native sentries round the house were relieved by Europeans, much to my satisfaction. A company of the 32nd went off to Cawnpore yesterday under Captain Lowe, also some irregular cavalry under Captain Barber. Captain Hayes accompanied the party as Sir Henry's agent.

22nd.—An attack was again expected. I drove to camp in the evening, and sat some time with John. I saw very little of him, as he seldom liked to be away from the regiment. In the middle of the night I was awakened by the cry, 'Turn out the guard!' and by a clatter of arms. I jumped up, fancying the house was attacked. Captain Mansfield (32nd) came down at once to see what was the matter, and found it was a false alarm. The state of suspense we lived in was very trying, but we felt thorough confidence in Sir Henry, whose energy, prudence, and forethought could not be exceeded, and we knew that every necessary precaution would be taken, and that all that human wisdom could do for our safety would be done. Captain Wilson (13th N.I.) was appointed adjutant-general; he laughed at the idea of a mutiny.

23rd.—Mrs. Case and I drove to camp in the morning, and saw the scene of last night's fire, a large empty outhouse. Had the wind been high, and had the flames spread, the building being in a direct line with the mess-house of the 13th N.I., where a company of the 32nd was located, and with Sir Henry's house, the consequences might have been serious ; and this looked as if the fire had been more intentional than accidental. This day a rising was also expected ; and Colonel Case, who was far from being an alarmist, advised our having a bundle of necessaries ready, in case we might have to leave our present quarters suddenly. We followed his advice, and communicated it to the other ladies in the house. News arrived from Cawnpore that Sir Hugh Wheeler, commanding there, had fully expected the native troops to rise, but the danger had been averted for the time. Telegraphic messages were constantly passing ; it was thought that as long as Cawnpore remained quiet Lucknow was safe. Sir Henry ordered that all the roofs of the bungalows, which were thatched, and therefore easily ignited, should be kept constantly wetted in case of fire.

Sunday, 24th.—A quiet day. I went to camp in the morning, and to the cantonment church in the evening. During the service one or two shots were fired, apparently very close to us. For an instant I felt much alarmed, but soon remembered that the great Mussulman fast called Ramazan ended to-day, and that when the new moon appears, which ushers in the festival, guns are fired off to salute it. Two or three gentlemen left the church, but soon returned; and Sir Henry did not even turn his head, so we felt quite reassured. Mr. Polehampton preached a beautiful sermon, one most applicable to the time and our position.

25*th*.—I was awakened very early this morning by John, who told me all the ladies were to go at once to the city Residency, commonly called the Bailie Guard. Sir Henry, having received a telegraphic message from Cawnpore, 'All quiet now, but not expected to remain so,' thought it advisable that all the women and children should be placed in comparative safety before the rising here, which was hourly expected, should take place. We were soon ready, and left cantonments in no happy mood, as it was a great trial to us all to be parted from our husbands. I drove to the city in the buggy, the children following in the bullock carriage; the road was occupied by cavalry, and everything wore a most warlike appearance. The Gubbinses kindly asked me to stay in their house, which was inside the Residency walls; and I was reluctantly compelled to part company with Mrs. Case and her sister, who occupied the Residency house. Our party consisted of Major and Mrs. Banks and one child, Mr. and Mrs. Thornhill, Mr. and Mrs. Polehampton, Mrs. Cooper and two children, Mrs. Brydon and two children.

During the day I received one or two notes from John, saying that better news had arrived, and he still hoped we might escape the horrors of a revolt. I went over to the Residency house in the evening, and walked on the roof with Mrs. Case and her sister. The place was filled with women and children; all seemed very crowded and uncomfortable. Everything was being prepared within the Residency walls to sustain a siege, cartloads of provisions and grain, ammunition, etc., coming in continuously. Two large guns were placed in position, pointing down the road leading to cantonments, and it was very evident preparations for the worst were being made. Whilst we were at dinner to-night, Mr. Gubbins received a telegraphic message from Sir Hugh Wheeler. He said they had passed an anxious night; but all had remained quiet, and he trusted the crisis was past.

For the next few days everything remained quiet. Mrs. Case and I generally drove to cantonments in the afternoon, and sat with our husbands under a semianah (awning), which they had pitched in camp. These visits were a great treat to us; but we were obliged to return to the city before dusk, and even with this precaution I do not think our driving down each day by ourselves was very prudent. There were a great many ill-looking men about; and I was always very glad when we had re-crossed the iron bridge dividing us from cantonments. I was the coachman, and drove at a pretty good pace. All in camp led a most trying, fatiguing, and anxious life; constant alarms and reports kept them continually on the alert, and rest was almost out of the question. Sir Henry himself directed and inspected all things; his energy and activity were unsurpassed. Night and day seemed all the same to him. Either encouraging the wavering, punishing the rebellious, rewarding the faithful, visiting the Sepoy lines to show his confidence in them, giving audience to influential natives, or examining our own defences, all the energies of his master mind were employed in the one great effort of deferring the coming catastrophe, which he clearly saw was inevitable, and thereby rendering us better prepared to meet it; and doubtless but for him, and God's blessing on his endeavours, the fate of all in Lucknow would have been but a prelude to the horrors of Cawnpore. John generally accompanied him in his visits to the city and Muchee Bowun; the latter was a fort three miles from the Residency, occupied by a company of the 32nd and some native troops, and it was munitioned and provisioned to stand a siege. About this time some men were caught in the lines of the 71st N.I., said to have come over from Delhi, trying to induce the Sepoys to desert to the rebel army, promising them high pay and promotion. The 71st themselves showed the traitors up; and the adjutant, Mr. Chambers, came to the lines to arrest them. One of them attempted to shoot him, but was overpowered, and the next day sentenced to be hanged. The Sepoys were very handsomely rewarded.

29*th.*—Drove down to camp as usual. I had had a visit from John in the morning, and did not think him at all in good spirits. Mrs. Case and I were mentioning some report we had heard about a mutiny at Peshawur, and rather laughing at its absurdity. He checked us by saying, 'It's no laughing matter; the most dreadful reports reach us daily. You think the crisis is past; I tell you it is yet to come.' From that hour I seemed to realize the true seriousness of our position, and could never again smile at anything I heard, feeling that, if not true then, it might be before long.

30th.—We spent some hours in camp this afternoon, and John and Colonel Case accompanied us a short distance on our way home; we little thought then what perils shortly awaited them. I went to my room that night earlier than usual, and was just going to bed, when Mr. Gubbins knocked at my door, and said, 'Bring your children, and come up to the top of the house immediately.' I dressed myself and them, and obeyed as quickly as possible. I found all the inmates of the house assembled on the roof, and looking anxiously towards cantonments, where fires were blazing in all directions, and from whence cannonading and musketry firing could plainly be heard. Mr. Polehampton offered up a prayer for our preservation, and for those engaged in the strife, and then all the men prepared to defend our position, should it be attacked. Guns, revolvers and ammunition were plentiful, and we had some skilful matchlock men to assist us. If the house had been attacked, we were in a tolerably safe position against anything but artillery, as the roof was approached by a spiral staircase, up which but one could come at a time, and one good revolver could have kept the foe at bay for some time. A sowar (native horse soldier) arrived from cantonments with the news that the Sepoys had mutinied, and were burning and plundering in all directions. About twelve o'clock I received a note from John telling me all was over for the present. I was most thankful to see his handwriting, as my anxiety on his account had been great. All crowded round me to hear the news. He did not think the rising was general. Brigadier Handscomb and Captain Grant, 71st N.I., had been killed, also another officer. I sent the note to Mrs. Case, as her husband was mentioned in it. We all now felt reassured, and lay down to get a little rest—sleep was out of the question. At daylight we descended from the roof, but were startled by hearing heavy guns again.

Sunday, 31*st*.—I had a few lines from John this morning telling me a little of what had occurred last night. It appeared the nine o'clock gun was the signal, and as it fired the Sepoys seized their muskets and rushed on our guns. Spies had reported their intention to Sir Henry Lawrence, and therefore in an instant the 32nd was turned out ready to receive them. A little desultory firing ensued, but a few rounds of grape soon dispersed the rebels, who then scattered themselves about cantonments burning and plundering the houses. The remnants of the 13th, 48th, and 71st N.I. regiments, who remained faithful, were drawn up in line with the 32nd. Brigadier Handscomb was shot dead when imprudently venturing down the lines. Mr. Grant, 71st N.I., was murdered at the quarter-guard of his regiment. Mr. Chambers, adjutant, 13th N.I., was badly wounded, but saved by some of his own men, and escorted to the Residency. Cornet Raleigh, a young officer in the 7th Cavalry, was murdered. Mrs. Bruere, wife of the colonel of the 13th N.I., had a narrow escape. She was spending the night in cantonments contrary to orders, and while the mutineers were entering her house, some of the faithful Sepoys of the regiment got her out at the back, and hid her in the dry bed of a nullah (stream) until the morning. At daylight it was reported that the rebels had taken up a position near Moodkipore, where the 7th Cavalry were stationed. Leaving a small force in cantonments under Colonel Case, Sir Henry immediately gave them chase with the 32nd, under John, and some artillery and cavalry; but the latter did not show much alacrity in the pursuit, and some of them rode over to the enemy at once. The sun was very powerful, the men exhausted, and the Sepoys soon got out of their reach, excepting a few who were made prisoners. Finding the uselessness of the pursuit, the troops now marched back to cantonments. The destruction of property during the night had been terrible, but it was no time to be thinking of losses; preservation of life was the chief thought in our minds. At 12 o'clock (noon) Major Banks sent word there was a rising in the city he could not withstand, and we were again ordered up to the roof; but on second thoughts it was decided that it would be better for us all to go over to the Residency house. Over we went at once, and the confusion and excitement that prevailed there baffles description. We all anticipated the worst, and, indeed, if we had been attacked then, our resistance could have been but for a short time. A clerk had already been murdered in the city, showing the feeling that was abroad. To add to our uneasiness, we were told not to crowd too much together, as the building was not very strong, and it was feared would not stand so great a pressure. I took refuge with Mrs. Case and her sister, who occupied a room on the top floor. We were soon joined by Mrs. Halford and her daughter, who were in a state of the greatest misery and alarm. Their house had been burned and plundered. Colonel Halford, 71st N.I., soon afterwards arrived, and the meeting was most painful to witness. Towards evening we went on the roof of the house. Occasional shots could be heard, and we were told that a disturbance in the city had been attempted, but the native police had behaved well and put it down. I was beginning to feel very uneasy about the force in cantonments, when to my great joy we descried troops crossing the iron bridge, and soon recognised the 32nd, with Sir Henry and John at their head. When they came within the Residency walls Sir Henry made the troops a speech, which was loudly cheered. From this time the Residency, or Bailie Guard, as it was called, became his headquarters. A small force with four guns was left in cantonments under Colonel Case to keep the communication open. The Muchee Bowun fort was also occupied by our troops, Captain Francis, 13th N.I., in command. I saw John for a few minutes after he came in from cantonments. Mr. Polehampton and Mr. Harris, our chaplains, read the evening service to us, and then we were all glad to lie down and rest, after the excitement and anxiety of the past day and night. Our own room, or rather Mrs. Case's, was so oppressively hot and crowded, that Miss Dickson, the children and I slept on the roof of the house with some others. The night passed quietly.

June 1st.—As everything seemed to have quieted down in the city, those ladies who had been staying in the Gubbinses', Fayrers' and

Ommanneys' houses returned to their quarters. I preferred remaining with Mrs. Case and Miss Dickson. We had a scrambling breakfast, and finding that the present mode of living was likely to last for some time, we determined on organizing a sort of mess, instead of being entertained by Dr. and Mrs. Ogilvie, who had always occupied the Residency house with Sir Henry. Kind and hospitable as they were, they could not arrange comfortably for so many. I asked Mrs. Radcliffe and Mrs. Boileau, 7th Cavalry, with their six children, to join us, and made my khansamah (butler) cater for the party. All approved of the arrangement, and it certainly was much pleasanter. John took up his abode in a small room in the lower part of the house. Sir Henry gave him the command of the troops, an onerous and anxious position; but it showed the confidence he placed in him. He appointed as his A.D.C. Captain Birch, 71st N.I. He had been struck by the activity and intelligence of this young officer upon one or two occasions when he had acted orderly officer to him on field-days, and selected him on that account. After-events fully justified his choice. Mrs. Case heard from Colonel Case to-day; he wrote cheerfully, though he had suffered from Saturday's work. Our artillery had opened fire in such a reckless manner that the shot had gone right through his tent, killing two of his servants and two horses—really a very serious loss. I finished a long home letter to-day, and John sent it to Captain Barrow, who was at Salone, in Oude; but I believe it never reached him. There was a false alarm to-night, and the men rushed to the guns and lighted the port-fires, fancying the rebels were approaching.

June 2nd.—Miss Dickson and I dined with Sir Henry in his tent. He was most kind and hospitable, and insisted on all the members of his staff living at his table. Whilst at dinner the news arrived of the defeat of a body of rebels near Delhi by the 60th Rifles. He said it was refreshing to get some good news, and his spirits seemed quite raised. Sad news, however, also arrived of the death of the commander-in-chief, General Anson. It was attempted to keep this a secret, but it soon leaked out.

June 3rd.—We received the sad news to-day that Captain Hayes, Mr. Barber, and Mr. Fayrer, brother to Dr. Fayrer, had been murdered by their own escort near Mynpoorie. Mr. Gubbins communicated the dreadful intelligence to Mrs. Hayes; and in the evening, finding that Mrs. Barber was still in ignorance of what had occurred, I asked Mr. Polehampton to break it to her. She had only been married three months. Captain Hayes left five children. This was a very, very sad day. Accounts were daily received of mutinies and murders in the different districts of Oude, and some fugitives came in at this time from Seetapore, having escaped with difficulty, and undergone many hardships and dangers. News arrived that the troops at Cawnpore had mutinied on the 2nd, and were besieging our small force there, consisting of one company of the 32nd, under Captain Moore, principally married men, with their wives and children, a few of the 84th, and some artillery, all under the command of Sir Hugh Wheeler. We could learn no particulars. The soldiers who were sent from here to Cawnpore returned some days ago. Sir Hugh Wheeler, imagining that all danger was past, had sent them back, and actually offered *us* assistance.

Sunday, 7th.—We had service in the Residency church to-day. Mr. Polehampton always read prayers, morning and evening, in our house, which was a great comfort to us.

June 8th.—News arrived from Cawnpore describing the garrison there as being in great distress. We felt deeply anxious about them. There were three officers in Lucknow whose wives were in Cawnpore. One, Captain Evans, was in our house, and his wretched face used quite to haunt me. He seldom spoke.

9th.—Colonel Case came in from camp this morning; he was always so sanguine and cheery, that a visit from him raised our spirits. He was one who always looked on the bright side of things.

12th.—I sent a letter home to-day by Major Gall, who had volunteered to take despatches to Allahabad; he had entreated hard to go, though he knew what a great risk he ran. He started disguised as a native, and took some of his own men, native cavalry, with him, who professed the greatest fidelity. The police force mutinied to-day. Captain Orr, commandant, came to the Residency with the news; they went off without attempting to molest their officers. In the afternoon, a force went out under John, consisting of two companies 32nd, two guns, and some Sikh cavalry. The rebels had had so much time to themselves, and had employed it so well, that it was almost impossible to overtake them. It was a fearfully hot day, and the men were quite exhausted after marching eight miles. The artillery opened fire at a long distance, and the cavalry, led by Captain Forbes and Lieutenant Hutchinson of the engineers, charged and took some prisoners; and then the infantry being unable to support them, the pursuit was given up. Mr. Thornhill was slightly wounded, two Sikhs killed, and a few wounded. It was now late in the evening, and John gave the order to return. On their way back through the city an attempt was made to lead the force the wrong way; but John held on his course, and most fortunate it was that he did so, for from the very street he had been advised to go down a sharp musketry fire was opened, but the shots fell too far off to do any harm. I did not see John before he started on this expedition, and was naturally very anxious. Two 32nd men died of heat-apoplexy on the march. Mrs. Case, Miss Dickson, and I went to-day to see a poor wounded woman who had escaped from Seetapore, and was being taken care of by Mrs. Wilkinson, 32nd. She was a very nice-looking girl about eighteen, and had two bad wounds in her side. Her escape, with her little boy, had been most wonderful. Of her husband's fate she was ignorant. There were several other refugees in the lower part of the Residency house, where the 32nd women lived, and we gave them some clothes, of which they stood much in need.

13*th.*—Still no news. I paid Mrs. Cowper a visit to-day. Our conversation was, of course, entirely on the state of affairs here and in other places ; it was difficult to talk or think of anything else. I asked John at this time if he thought the enemy would attack us. He said it was his firm opinion that they would. I then said, 'Do you think we can hold out?' He answered, 'Our position is a bad one, and we shall have a hard struggle.' I was glad to know what one might expect, as it enabled us to prepare for the worst. Our life was a most wearisome one ; the heat was very great. It was impossible to read much ; but we occupied our time in making clothes for the refugees, and this employment was a comfort to

ABOUT THE EDITOR

Pramod K. Nayar teaches at the Department of English, University of Hyderabad. His works on British India include, *English Writing and India, 1600-1920* (2008), *The Great Uprising* (2007), *Colonial Voices* (2012), *The British Raj: Keywords* (2017) and *Indian Travel Writing in the Age of Empire* (Bloomsbury 2020). He has edited *The Trial of Bahadur Shah Zafar* (2007), *The Penguin 1857 Reader* (2007), *Days of the Raj* (2009), *Women in Colonial India* (5 volumes, 2013), *English Siege and Prison Writings* (2016), *Indian Travel Writing, 1830-1947* (5 volumes, 2016) and *Colonial Education in India* (5 volumes, 2019). Besides these, he has also published extensively on Human Rights and Literature, the graphic novel and celebrity culture.